the
year
of
the
buttered
cat

a mostly true story

Susan Haas with Lexi Haas

PENELOPE EDITIONS

PENELOPE EDITIONS is an imprint of Penny Candy Books
Young adult & middle grade books with guts & vision
www.penelopeeditions.com
Oklahoma City & Greensboro

 This book is printed on paper certified to the environmental and social standards of the Forest Stewardship Council™ (FSC®).

Photo of Susan & Lexi Haas: Susan Haas
Design & illustrations: Shanna Compton

Library of Congress Cataloging-in-Publication Data

Names: Haas, Susan Tyler, 1964- author. | Compton, Shanna, illustrator.
Title: The year of the buttered cat : a mostly true story / Susan Haas with
  Lexi Haas ; [illustration, Shanna Compton].
Description: Oklahoma City : Penelope Editions, 2021. | Audience: Ages
  10-14 | Audience: Grades 4-6
Identifiers: LCCN 2020056370 (print) | LCCN 2020056371 (ebook) | ISBN
  9781734225938 (hardcover) | ISBN 9781736031957 (epub) | ISBN
  9781736031957 (kindle edition) | ISBN 9781736031957 (pdf)
Subjects: LCSH: Haas, Lexi--Health. | Kernicterus--Patients--United
  States--Biography. | Brain--Surgery--Patients--United States--Biography.
  | Brain damage--Patients--United States--Biography.
Classification: LCC RC387.5 .H23 2021 (print) | LCC RC387.5 (ebook) | DDC
  617.4/81--dc23
LC record available at https://lccn.loc.gov/2020056370
LC ebook record available at https://lccn.loc.gov/2020056371

25 24 23 22 21   1 2 3 4 5

For Ken, Kali, Kasey, Hannah, and Tucker,
who have lived this story with us.
—SH and LH

"If all my possessions were taken from me with
one exception, I would choose to keep the power of
communication, for by it I would soon regain all the rest."

—Daniel Webster

"The ability to speak does not make you intelligent."

—Qui-Gon Jinn, *Star Wars: Episode I,*
The Phantom Menace

"The inability to speak does not make you unintelligent."

—me, Lexi Haas. Just now.

"I just know before this is over, I'm gonna
need a whole lot of serious therapy."

—Donkey, *Shrek*

CHAPTER 1
Age 13, 24 hours until surgery

After thirteen years and a bazillion appointments, I should be over my fear of doctors. I'm not. I hate how they try to chat you up like you're friends, then *bam!* Needle in the arm. Or worse, they leave the room, and when you start to breathe again, they send in someone else to do the dirty work.

I'm not afraid of all doctors. In the Marvel universe, Bruce Banner has like *seven* PhDs, and yeah, he goes all Hulk when he's ticked, but you don't see *him* chasing down kids with a needle.

For me, the bad guys are the *-ists*—neurologists, internists, anesthesiologists. *Those* types. The ones with the pokers.

So it's kinda twisted that this morning, I'm lying on a hospital gurney in Kansas City, Missouri. I'm a zillion miles from home. I'm wearing one of those gowns that barely covers my butt. And I *chose* to be here.

Today it's for "presurgical medical imaging"—basically a photo shoot for my brain. But tomorrow, 6 a.m. sharp, I'm back for the real thing. Elective brain surgery. My *second* elective brain surgery.

Elective, by the way, is medical talk for *one hundred-percent optional*. And also for *bring on the needles*. Like I said, it's kinda twisted.

Unfortunately, I have a gifted memory, so all my needle sticks are stored in my brain like hundreds of movie clips. But the only one that really matters is the one that's about to happen any minute.

There's a little opening between the curtains in my cubicle where I can see nurses, techs, and *-ists* marching around pre-op like stormtroopers on the Death Star.

I focus on breathing and—okay, don't laugh—squeezing my rock. It isn't an *actual* rock. *Obviously.* These people stripped every personal thing from me for "safekeeping" when I got here. But at least for now, they didn't take my memories, and that is what my rock is. The real one was a gift from my friend Anna when we were little kids. She pressed it in my hand and curled my fingers around it. I squeezed that rock until every bump, every corner, burned into my memory. Now, when I need to quiet my brain, I can go back and squeeze my hand hard enough, and the memory floods back. Nobody is gonna take *that* from me.

Mom must know I'm obsessing because she pulls the curtain closed and turns on my iPad. "How about some fanfic?

What goes best with long hospital waits—*Star Wars*? Marvel? Wizarding?"

Before I can answer, a nurse charges into my curtained cubicle. She slams into my wheelchair, sending my service dog, Gus, scrambling for a corner.

Perfect. The entire Galactic Empire is out there, and they send in Jar Jar Binks.

"Good morning! We'll get that IV started soon, but first, sign and date." She hands Mom a clipboard without even a glance towards me.

I take a deep breath and force air from my lungs. What comes out is *ggguuhhh*. It sounds like a pencil sharpener. Or an angry dog. Or maybe an angry dog sharpening a pencil.

I'm guessing the nurse has gone with "angry dog." She spins around and looks at me like I might bite.

"That growl means no," Mom says. "I think she wants to sign the release herself."

The nurse clears her throat. "Sorry, sweetie, this has to be signed by an adult. Are you over eighteen?"

She knows the answer. Not only am I "fun-sized" as my brother and sisters say, this is a *children's* hospital.

I growl again. *Ggguuhhh*.

"I didn't think so," the nurse says.

"How about if we both sign it?" Mom asks. She smooths my long, dark braids.

I stick out my tongue. The nurse narrows her eyes.

"Tongue out means yes," Dad says, glancing up from his phone.

"Excuse me?"

Dad shrugs. "She came up with those herself when she was a little kid. The growl thing means no, and sticking her tongue out means yes."

Usually, I add in my head. *It USUALLY means yes. Sometimes it doesn't.*

The nurse nods and smiles—a bright, happy, totally fake smile.

Dad props me against his shoulder. Mom puts the pen in my hand and holds my wrist steady. I write *Lexi Haas*.

Underneath, Mom writes *Susan*. When the nurse coughs, Mom adds our last name.

"Alrighty then," the nurse says. Her lips purse so thin they all but disappear into her face. "Someone will be in soon for that IV."

I know what she's thinking. What *everyone* is thinking. *You're doing this AGAIN? The last one either didn't work or something went horribly wrong.*

Okay. Fair enough. But here's the thing: it did work. Sort of.

Before the first operation six years ago, I could control exactly two muscles—one that extended my pointer finger and one that stuck out my tongue. Since then, with lots of help, I can walk. If someone holds my wrist steady, I can even play video games.

My voice is better too. Before, I only had a few sounds I could make on purpose. Of course, there was my *ggguuhhh*. When I got excited, that got all high-pitched and sounded exactly like Chewbacca, which was amazing, but I couldn't control it. Besides that, I had a squeal, a groan, and (#humblebrag) an impressively loud burp when I hyperventilated. Sometimes, out of the blue, I would blurt out a completely clear word or two, but I had zero control over when that would happen. Boy did *that* lead to some interesting situations.

Now, if I suck in air until my lungs are about to burst, then let it out nice and slow, I can usually puff out a couple of words before I'm out of breath. It's a neat trick, but so far only my family can understand me, and when I'm tired—like this morning—it doesn't work at all.

"Good morning!" a new nurse says. "I'm here to go over tomorrow's procedure and get Lexi's IV started."

She's pushing a cart so big that it swallows my cubicle.

Gus dives between Dad's legs and lets out a very loud fart. He does that sometimes when he's nervous.

"Oh . . . Wow," Dad says, putting a hand over his mouth and nose. "We can't even crack a window."

The cart makes me nervous too, but I can't help but laugh.

New nurse pulls up a page on her computer and starts to read about "tomorrow's procedure." I tune out. They're going into a different part of my brain, but otherwise it's the same surgery as last time so I know how it's going down:

The surgeon will drill a hole in my skull. He'll drop in two wires, and over the course of eight to ten hours steer them towards the center of my brain, which I know, I *know* sounds more like ice fishing than brain surgery. Then he'll connect those wires to a stimulator implanted in my stomach, and that stimulator will send constant electric pulses up to my thalamus.

For the rest of my life.

Oh, and there's one other thing. I'll be awake while they do it.

For the surgeon to hit the millimeters-wide spot in my brain with the millimeters-wide electrodes on the end of those wires, the doctors have to ask me questions during surgery. And I have to answer.

"Lexi, can you move your hand?" and I'll wiggle my finger.

"Lexi, can you open and close your eyes?" and I'll blink.

"Lexi, do you feel any strange sensation?" and I'll point to the card that says "No," but in my head, I'll add, *Nothing but the ice fishing contest going on up there.*

"Any questions?" New nurse asks me.

I'm guessing she's asked more than once, because Mom is poking me in the ribs.

Ggguuhhh.

"No," Mom interprets. "She doesn't."

"Then let's get on with that IV. I just need to peek at your ID band first."

She picks up my wrist and examines the plastic bracelet I got when I checked in this morning.

"Charlotte, North Carolina! You're a long way from home, aren'tcha?"

I stick out my tongue as Mom launches into the explanation I've already heard three times today. She'll tell her it's because of Steve Shapiro.

The nurse's eyes will brighten, and she'll say, "You mean *Doctor* Shapiro? As in *Head of Neurology* Doctor Shapiro?"

Mom will nod and tell her how Steve has been my doctor since I was a baby.

What she probably won't say is that she and Dad have brought me out here every year since he left the East Coast. She definitely won't tell her that once you find an *-ist* you trust you don't let something silly like a half a country stand in your way. I wish she would.

As Mom talks, I turn my attention to the cart. There's a computer monitor and next to that, a stuffed bear wearing scrubs.

That bear is for sure a decoy. A small peace offering before they inflict pain. In fact, it should be right about . . . *Bingo.* On a small tray, sticking out from under a surgical cloth. The needle. I'm thirteen. Why do they think they can fool me with a toy?

"Someone will turn off her stimulator before the MRI, right? Because that has to be done. It has to be off before she enters the MRI." Mom's pacing while she talks.

New nurse is tapping away on her keyboard. She doesn't look up but nods and smiles. I bet she's thinking, *You've already told five people, lady. Just chill.*

But Mom will never chill. Not in the hospital. Not in the *-ist* factory. She'll check and recheck every chart entry, every order. She's a medical writer, and dad's a chiropractor, but the funny thing is, they don't like *-ists* any more than I do.

Dad, however, is pretty much always chill. He's slouched in a purple recliner scrolling through his phone with his T-shirt pulled up over his nose as a fart filter. He has jumped out the window via the internet.

His phone pings. He stares at it for a second then sits up straight.

"Of your thousands of friends, Lexi, every single one seems to have an opinion about this surgery. I'll bet you'll never guess what this one says."

Okay. Let's get one thing straight: I do *not* have thousands of friends. Online I have a few thousand Facebook and Twitter *followers* who have been around since my first surgery. In that world I'm well known, kinda like a popular girl in a big school, but who really knows that girl? Who's really *friends* with her?

In the real world, I'm homeschooled. I have Anna and Elle Trejo, who are sisters, and of course *my* three sisters, Kali, Kasey, and Hannah, and my brother, Tucker, and maybe a few other close friends. Other than that, I'm practically invisible. When you sit below everyone and can't talk, it's easy for people to forget you're even there. But online, especially if your Dad posts pictures of Every. Move. You. Make. (insert grimace emoji), you pop up on feeds and *ta-da!* Like Harry Potter pulling off his invisibility cloak, people see you. And when they see you, they have opinions.

Still, I need those messages. For one thing, while I'm here, Facebook is the only way I can talk to Anna and Elle. I'm pretty sure we are the last three teenagers on the planet who don't have cell phones yet. Our moms say we don't need them (double grimace emoji).

I uncurl a finger to point at Dad's phone.

Dad clears his throat. "Claudia in New Hampshire writes, 'Why would you put this sweet girl through this again?'"

I arch and my arm flails. I'm not sweet, I'm thirteen, and this was my decision.

Gus swoops in like he's having a superhero fantasy. He leaps on the gurney, plops his sixty-five pounds across my chest, and drapes a paw over my arm.

He smiles at me—I swear he does smile—and thumps his thick, black tail as if to say, "Stopped the arm before it took over Gotham. You're welcome."

I laugh. This dog has a problem with personal space, but he's great for distraction.

New nurse makes a final, dramatic strike on her keyboard then claps her hands. "I'll grab a tourniquet, and we'll get that IV underway. Oh, this is for you!"

She tucks the bear in the crook of my arm. The curtain billows behind her like a cape. In my head, I hum the Darth Vader theme song.

"Well, tons of people care about this girl, and I get it, but I don't even know where to start with that message," Mom says. She puts the bear back on the cart.

Truth. Where to start. Every part gets under my skin. I will not be the little disabled girl who people *do stuff to.* Or be pitied like I'm some sort of Tiny Tim.

"They're just concerned," Dad says. "I think everyone wants to know what we—what *she*—expects from this surgery and that she's . . . you know, managing expectations."

Managing expectations? I've had a lifetime of that! Twenty-four hours before elective brain surgery is not the time for "cautious optimism." It's the time to let your imagination race around the hospital like a wild, bucking filly, daring anyone to try and harness it, because that's what gets you through. That's what allows you to roll through the operating room doors while your parents hold each other and wave goodbye. Without raging optimism, no one would be able to do these last twenty-four hours.

I'm flailing again, and Gus is having a tough time figuring out which limb to stop first.

Mom grabs my leg. "Ken, maybe now isn't the time for this discussion."

New nurse is back, holding a blue elastic cord and alcohol swabs. She picks up my arm and thumps at the vein near my wrist like Mom does when she's picking cantaloupe at the grocery store. She ties the tourniquet near my elbow and thumps some more.

Gus edges closer and licks my hand. He knows what comes next.

New nurse tears open an alcohol prep pad, and a familiar, prickly odor overwhelms the cubicle. My eyes water. It's only partly from the smell. For me, isopropyl alcohol is a prepackaged, premeasured dose of confrontation. It reminds me of where I've been, where I need to go, and what I have to do.

I want to dive under the table, but *obviously* I can't, so I dive into my thoughts. *Why ARE you doing this again? People want to know! I want to know!*

There's my joke answer—I want to walk and talk and beat my brother at Minecraft—but that's the answer I give when I don't want to get into the real reason, the real story. That story goes way back—much further than this surgery or even the last one. The real story honestly began when *I* began.

In my earliest days, something terrible happened—something criminal. It left me with this crazy body. And without a voice. It would be years before I pieced together the evidence and learned the truth.

The cold alcohol pad hits my wrist. The sharp smell jabs at me. *Hurry, hurry. Tell this now. Before tomorrow. Before you roll back to surgery. So much can happen in there.*

C'mon, Lexi, *focus*. The real reason involves a prophecy, a theft, a buttered cat, and, most of all, an Epic Reasoning Fail. But before all that were the fragmented memories of my earliest days.

"Okay, Sweetie. You're going to feel a little stick . . ."

Deep breath in. My story. My evidence. Breath out.

CHAPTER 2
Before Age 2, Memories

Everyone has memories. No ... wait. *Nearly* everyone. There are people who get sick or injured and wake up without a memory. I keep reminding myself that this rarely happens. Also rare: people who can remember everything. And *that* is me. My family knows my memory is basically my superpower, but even they don't know the whole of it.

The fact is, from age two, I can remember everything that has ever happened to me. Everything I have seen. Everything I have read. Everything.

This superpower or gift or whatever you want to call it showed up, out of the blue, around my second birthday. Remembering everything makes you a fast learner. The first thing you learn is that you do *not* want to remember everything. The second thing you learn is how to tune stuff out. Some people confuse this with Attention Deficit Disorder. It's not. It's Active Nonremembering. And it's a skill, not a disorder, thank you very much.

My memory before age two is a different story. It's not a totally blank page, but it's pretty close. What I do "remember" from before age two is mostly fake: stories my family has told over and over until they seem real.

One is about the morning after I was born. It was early spring in Charlottesville, Virginia. While my parents filled out discharge papers, my five-year-old brother, Tucker, stole my hospital bassinet. He drove me—a yellowed, wrinkly, and seriously *un*cute newborn—around the maternity ward like he was a NASCAR driver. A nurse ran after him saying, "That's not safe, young man!"

For years, this was the only story I ever heard about my birth. There were plenty of stories of the other kids, my four older siblings. When we sat around the dinner table and my parents talked about our earliest days, there was documentary-level information about everyone else's births. Just not mine.

I had one other fake memory. This one was about Luke, the yellow lab we had when I was a kid. Luke was the only dog I've ever known who had his own pet, a cat we affectionately named The Cat. I was only a year old when Luke got his cat, but my family told that story so often I could picture it.

We were visiting my grandparents in Georgia when Luke found a pile of greasy wrappers behind a dumpster. He sniffed the pile—and it jumped. The wrappers fell away, uncovering a tiny gray kitten. Luke lay down and licked that kitten top to bottom. The kitten must have decided that Luke was his mother because he pushed his paws back and forth on Luke's belly and tried to nurse. From a dog. A *boy* dog.

Mom was not a cat person, but even she couldn't say no to their sweet friendship. When we left for home the next day, the kitten came too. After a couple of days, Luke had licked away the kitten's buttery coating. When that was gone, he completely lost interest.

The kitten grew into a cat. By the time my memory came in full-on a year later, The Cat was a cranky little monster with mommy issues. He spent most of his day outside hunting mice and terrorizing neighborhood birds. But when Luke came back inside from a walk or pee break, The Cat would race inside behind him. He would try to nurse, and when that didn't work out, he'd find a spot nearby to watch Luke. The Cat was a stalker.

He was also awesome for Active Nonremembering. From my beanbag chair I would make a game of trying to find his green eyes peeking out from behind the TV stand or under a tent of old newspapers. It's impossible to pay attention to other stuff when you're hunting a Ninja cat. One hundred-percent impossible.

I wish I could say that the fake memories of The Cat and NASCAR Tucker were all my memories from my first two years. If they had been, everything would have been fine. Chances are, there would have been no Epic Reasoning Fail and no Year of the Buttered Cat. But they weren't the only ones.

I also had a random collection of broken memories, short snippets of life that for some reason stuck in my brain. And it was three of *those* memories that started all the trouble.

Snippet #1: I'm lying naked on an exam table in some -*ist*'s office. Mom's trying to diaper me, but I'm flipping and flopping like a fish on a boat dock. Finally, Mom throws down the diaper and covers her face with her hands.

A nurse hugs her and says, "Don't worry. She might catch up."

Snippet #2: I'm on Mom's lap, and my family is singing me the birthday song. Dad holds up my cake so I can see the single candle stuck in the middle. My body twists the opposite direction.

My sister, Hannah, says, "Make a wish, Lexi!" and Mom starts to cry.

Dad leans in and whispers, "She *will* catch up! I promise."

Snippet #3: I'm propped on pillows on my parents' bed. Dad is playing his guitar, strumming a jazz tune, "Summertime."

He reaches out and picks up my hand, which pulls back hard to my chest. He gently shakes my arm, and my muscles relax. He pulls my hand forward and strums his guitar. Three times. As my fingers brush the strings he sings, "You'll. Catch. Up."

By the time my total-recall memory came in when I was two, no one was talking about catching up any more. It didn't matter. These broken memories had lodged in my brain, taken root, and grown to a ginormous oak. *Don't worry. I'll catch up.*

If I had had a little brother or sister to watch, maybe I would've figured it out sooner, but I was the youngest. I had no idea how a kid learned to move or talk. Maybe *everyone* started with a body like mine. I just needed to be patient and wait for the delivery of my fully operational body. After all, my memory had magically appeared. My body would too. *Obviously.*

My body was coming. Soon. It would be arriving any time. Epic. Reasoning. Fail. And I could not let it go.

CHAPTER 3
Age 4, Discoveries

For three years, I waited for the delivery of my body. It did not come. Then the winter before I turned five, I discovered I had a second unusual talent, and for a little while, my focus shifted from something missing to something found.

Twice a week, I went to an "inclusive preschool"—a school that combined kids who walked and talked with kids who were "developing at their own pace," as they liked to say. But now it was time to start thinking about kindergarten. To help my parents understand our choices, two ladies from the state came to our house to test me.

That morning, Mom let me pick my outfit. I chose sparkly red cowgirl boots and a hand-me-down Spider-Man costume. When you have an older brother who's bananas for action and fantasy and magic, you get loads of characters and costumes handed down.

When our guests arrived, Luke bolted onto the porch with his tail wagging. The ladies stood up stiff and straight.

"Oh, aren't you . . . big," said one of the ladies.

I tried to wave, tried to move *only* an arm up and down like I practiced in therapy, but the excitement was too much. My whole body jerked. My leg kicked hard, and when it did, one of the boots flew off, sailing onto the porch. The ladies stared at it, sparkly in the morning sun.

"Please. Come in," said Mom.

She recovered my boot, then whistled for Luke. He trotted in with The Cat close behind.

The ladies introduced themselves as Roxanne And Betty From The State.

Betty looked me over. "Well, aren't you the cutest little . . . Wonder Girl!"

Wonder Girl? I flailed, and my other boot flew off, hitting Betty in the chest. She smiled thinly, handed it back to Mom, and smoothed her blue, wool skirt.

"Spider-Man," Mom corrected. "She wants you to know she's Spider—"

But the ladies had already wandered into the den.

Mom blew a strand of auburn hair from her face and positioned me in my beanbag chair. Luke plopped at my feet.

"Are you ready for some special tests, Lexi?" Roxanne asked.

I stuck out my tongue. The ladies flinched.

"Oh, sorry. Tongue out means yes," Mom said.

Betty smiled her thin smile.

"She came up with that herself," Mom offered.

"Shall we get started then? You'll want this in place before summer." She took out a notepad for herself and handed one to Roxanne.

"First, let's talk about skills. Preschoolers develop at different rates, but normally by Lexi's age they can answer questions and follow directions. They run, hop, kick . . ."

A streak of gray fur darted behind the couch. A second later, a pair of green eyes peeked around the corner. As my imagination heated up, my arms began to tingle.

Green Goblin! I'm sure he's up to no good. Sorry, Roxanne And Betty From The State. I need to check this out.

If I can fire my web-shooter at just the right angle . . . Thwak!

Yes! Ceiling fan carousel! Yahooo!

Dismount in three . . . two . . . one . . . now! Double twisting backflip and I'm on the couch, easy peasy.

Green Goblin leaps towards me. "You've spun your last web, Spider-Man!"

"Not so fast!"

Thwak!

Betty smacked her notebook against her palm, jolting me from my fantasy. She paced the room, stopping every few steps to tug at her skirt or scratch her leg.

"Please understand, Ms. Haas. This coming year is crucial to Lexi's development. Her motor skills are severely lacking. Her preschool teachers report that she doesn't interact much with her peers. If you ever want her to be included in school—in *life*—you need to accept the severe deficits she's dealing with. The district can't simply . . ."

You know you want to scratch your butt. C'mon, Betty, scratch it. Go ahead, Scratch. Your. Butt.

I was working on my telepathy, like Professor X from the X-Men.

I didn't care one nickel what Betty From The State thought I needed. A few weeks earlier Mom and I had made one of those closed terrariums from an empty jam jar. We put in dirt and moss and stuff then sealed it up. We didn't have to add anything to that jar, not even water, and everything in it was growing—*thriving*, Mom had written with me in a notebook.

Well, it was thriving until Luke chased The Cat, and The Cat knocked it off the table and smashed it to smithereens. Anyway, my house plus my family made my terrarium. They were all I needed to *thrive*.

"I think Lexi can read," Mom blurted.

"What?" Betty asked, blinking.

"Read. I think she can read."

Betty walked over and stared at me, like she was peeking inside an abandoned house to see if it could be salvaged, if it was worth saving.

"What makes you think that?"

Mom pointed to an old metal cookie sheet filled with plastic magnetic preschool letters. Before I was even a year old, if Mom held my body tight and my wrist steady, I could drag letters around that sheet and spell. It was my favorite game, so we spent hours every day learning new words.

Betty picked up the cookie sheet. "Lexi, can you spell your name for me?"

I stuck out a shaky finger and slid **Lexi** to the bottom.

"How about cat?" asked Roxanne.

cat

I smiled. *Bring on those special tests.*

After a few rounds of baby words, Mom interrupted. "Lexi, spell 'there' as in 'There it is'."

there

"Spell 'their' as in, 'This is their ball'."

their

"How about 'they're' the contraction?"

theyapostr

"Whoops! You've got off track. Let's try again!" Roxanne said, and she reached toward the letters.

Mom stopped her hand. "Let her finish."

theyapostrophere

The ladies frowned. Mom separated the letters a little.

They apostrophe re

"Umm . . . no punctuation in the starter set," Mom said, smiling.

Betty closed her book, crossed her knees, then uncrossed them. She tapped the notebook with her pen. "Ms. Haas, we don't have proper tools to measure this child's intelligence, but clearly she is very, very bright."

"Special," I wanted to say, but I could only grin and drool.

"It's highly unusual for a typical child to have language skills like these at her age," Betty said. "But for a child who can't talk, a child with such obvious physical deficits . . ."

C'mon, Betty. Go ahead. Scratch. Your. Butt . . .

That evening as I lay in bed, I could hear the soft hum of my parents' conversation in the room next door. Over the years, I had learned to pick up classified information by listening through the wall. Most nights, all I heard was Dad strumming his guitar before bedtime, but once in a while, I heard more. I was proud to be the first kid to know our grocery bill was gonna put us in the poor house, wherever that was. And the time Tucker tried to bring home a neighborhood cat, I was first to know that *thank* God it turned out to be our neighbor's fully vaccinated house cat.

And that night, after the kindergarten transition meeting, I overheard Mom say, "With her skills, I just don't think regular school is an option."

Soon after, I started homeschool.

All my siblings had been homeschooled at some point or other. Most homeschooling families in Charlotte wanted a Christian education that they couldn't get in public schools. But that wasn't us at all. Mom always said we just needed *other* stuff we couldn't get in public schools.

Kali and Kasey had eventually gone back to regular school, but Hannah and Tucker were still at home. Adding one more kid at the kitchen table wasn't a big deal. School was easy for me, and by summer vacation that year I was ready for second grade.

I started the summer of my fifth year overflowing with confidence. This would be the year my body would be coming in. *Obviously.* My memory and language skills were my super powers. Once I got my body and my voice, life would be amazing. What could go wrong?

CHAPTER 4
Age 13, 22 hours until surgery

I'm gonna let you in on a secret. There are times that I'm glad people can't understand me. And this is one of them.

New nurse has tried eight times to hit the vein for my IV. She started with my right hand, and now she's fishing around in the left. I'm huffing out curse words every time she shifts the needle. She has no clue I'm swearing.

Dad snorts, because he knows what I'm saying. Mom usually gives me the stink eye when I curse, but this time she doesn't. She holds my arm steady, and I can see her grimacing.

Finally, she closes her eyes and says, "Please go find someone who can hit her vein."

New nurse pulls out the needle, mumbles an apology, and disappears around the curtain.

Dad holds up his phone. "So, do you want to answer Claudia in New Hampshire?"

Mom pulls out my old cookie sheet. Yeah, *that* cookie sheet. It's *mega* embarrassing, but when I'm wiped, I can't talk any other way. Back home, I have a computerized communication device, but I still don't have enough muscle control to use it for talking.

Mom sits me up and holds my wrist. I extend a shaky finger and drag letters until it reads: **My real friends will understand.**

That's all I can manage. I slump onto her shoulder.

Dad's phone pings so I know he sent the message.

Dad is my "official" social media liaison. Six years ago, before my first surgery, Mom and I were away a lot with appointments. Dad had to stay in Charlotte to work and watch my brother and sisters, but here's the thing—my dad is not a bystander. He had to *do* something, so he set up my website and Facebook page.

Soon after, the media started. I was the first person ever with my condition to have this procedure, and the world loves firsts. There were stories in the local news, then the national news, and before long, there were thousands of people all over the world following my progress.

The thing about this procedure is that it unfolds slowly, like a lopsided three-act play.

First act is surgery. It has nearly all the drama, but it's over in a day.

Second act is recovery from surgery. Ten days with fading action.

Third act gets most of the stage time, but it's the part where you fall asleep and then clap politely when it's over. Act three is programming the stimulator so it sends the right set of instructions to my brain. Changes are made a little at a time, so this part can take months—even years.

The totally insane thing is that even after waiting years for the curtain call, my audience never left. My Facebook "friends" have continued watching and cheering me on. Usually, my social media . . . ummm . . . *presence*—yeah, I guess that's the word for it—usually, it doesn't bother me, but sometimes, I just want to be a regular kid. Even a regular disabled kid.

A different nurse pokes her head into my cubicle. This one doesn't have a needle in her hand, and she doesn't make a move in my direction.

"I just wanted to give you a head's up. There's a delay for the MRI. We have a baby with a CVA who's been triaged, so sit tight. We'll keep you posted."

The nurse leaves, and Mom shakes her head. "A baby with a stroke!"

At *stroke*, I jump. Gus shifts to hold me down.

"How heartbreaking for those parents! At least they're in good hands." She pauses then adds, "They can't hit a vein, but this hospital knows how to butter the whole cat."

Dad and I laugh because we know what she means is, "This hospital goes above and beyond."

I stare into Mom's eyes and open my mouth wide.

"I'm sure you're hungry and thirsty. As soon as we're done, you can get whatever you want from the cafeteria. But you know the hospital rules."

I know, I know. Nothing to eat or drink before they knock you out.

They're gonna put me to sleep to take pictures but keep me awake for surgery. How messed up is that?

"Why don't we text the kids and let them know what's going on," Dad says. "What do you want to tell them?"

I know he's trying to distract me by messaging my brother and sisters, but I won't bite. I stare at him with my open mouth.

He types something then reads it out loud. "'The MRI is delayed because of an emergency. Lexi wants you to know she's starving.' Is that okay?"

I stick out my tongue.

After a few minutes, Dad's phone pings again, but this one is a little different from the Facebook ping. Dad is a gadget freak and has worked out different tones for texts, emails, and Facebook messages. And this one is the text ping.

He holds the phone so I can read it.

It's my oldest sister, Kali: *Sorry, Lex! That stinks!*

Another text pops up. This time, it's my second oldest

sister, Kasey: *Bummer! Make Mom and Dad get you a nice lunch to make up for skipping breakfast!*

Now one from Hannah: *Try to think about something else. Any cute male nurses on the floor?*

I laugh at that and wait for the fourth ping. And wait. *Always late to the party.*

After a few minutes, it finally comes. Tucker has sent two pictures. The first is of his breakfast of eggs, toast, and fruit. The second is of him, eating it.

Jerk. I smile.

I miss them so much. They're sprinkled around the country in colleges and grad schools. Tucker was last, heading off to California last fall. It's so weird not having them here.

They're coming to visit after I get home from surgery. Tucker is even coming to Kansas City to fly back with us. It's not the same as having them here now. They're a huge part of my life. In fact, if it weren't for them, there would never have been a Year of the Buttered Cat. Which reminds me . . . Deep breath in. My story. Breath out.

CHAPTER 5
Age 5, The Year of the Buttered Cat

The Year of the Buttered Cat was more than a year. It was actually thirteen months. And it wasn't just about a buttered cat. The Cat would probably argue otherwise, but he's the arguing kind. As far as names go it's not great, but in the years after, as I looked back and tried to make sense of it all, that was the name that popped into my head, so it stuck. And it never mattered because, until now, no one else knew it happened, let alone that it had a name.

It all began one late July day the summer I was five and all because of *Finding Nemo*.

That Friday, Mom had a deadline with her medical writing. Normally, my brother and sisters watched me, but Kali and Kasey were away with friends until Sunday, and Hannah and Tucker were MIA. Mom propped me on my beanbag chair, popped in *Finding Nemo*, and went to work at her desk.

When Dad came home, he stretched out on his back next to me, and we watched the end together. When Marlin sent

Nemo off to fish school, Dad leaned against my shoulder and cried. He always cries at stuff like that.

Finally, he sat up and wiped his face.

"You've never been to the ocean, have you?"

Ggguuhhh. I arched hard.

I had wanted to go for *forever*. Every year, someone would tell me about the beach, about the sand and the waves. It was only a four-hour drive from Charlotte, but I had never seen it in person.

Dad looked at me for a long minute, then grabbed my hand and kissed it. "Tomorrow, we're going. Tomorrow, you're gonna see the ocean, even if it's just for the day."

The next morning, my parents loaded the van with *Harry Potter* CDs and a cooler of sandwiches and drove me, Hannah, and Tucker to the beach. By the time we got there, my legs ached.

Dad lifted me from my car seat and carried me down to the surf, leaving a trail of shoes and socks in the sand. He walked us straight out into the water in our clothes, not stopping until we were up to Dad's waist. Mom stood on the shore, holding up my bathing suit, but Dad and I just stared out into the bigness of it all. And this time, I cried. Everyone always says I'm a lot like my dad.

I spent the rest of that day splashing with Mom out in the

water, then on the shoreline on Dad's lap, squealing as waves crashed over us. Later, Mom wrapped me in a towel, blue-lipped and shivering, and I swatted down sandcastles Hannah and Tucker built for me.

I watched Tucker cartwheel down the beach, spinning faster and faster until he collapsed on his back in the sand. I made a promise. *When my body comes in, I'm gonna do that too.*

Finally, a late afternoon storm rolled in. Dad threw me over his shoulder and made a dash for the van.

On the drive home, my stomach rumbled. I flailed until Tucker looked up, then stared at him with an open mouth.

"Lexi's hungry," he said, "and I am too."

"Me three," said Hannah, staring into the empty cooler.

Dad's eyes flickered over us in the rearview mirror. "I'll find someplace to stop."

"Our budget doesn't include restaurants," Mom said quietly.

Dad pointed to a Shoney's billboard. "It's either this or listen to complaining the rest of the way home."

We dived on the Shoney's buffet like mosquitoes on flesh. At our table, Mom cradled me in her lap and scooped sweet potato into my mouth. Halfway through second helpings, a voice rang out behind us.

"What's wrong with the bay bee?"

Dad coughed into his fist but didn't look up.

"What's wrong with the bay bee?" the voice said again, this time louder.

Bay bee. Bay bee. I repeated it in my head, playing with the rhythm. Then it clicked. Baby. Was he talking about *me*? I arched and groaned.

Mom squeezed my leg and glanced behind us. "*Nothing*. Nothing is wrong with her."

"Can I please pray for the bay bee?"

Dad glanced at Mom. She gave a tiny shrug. Dad took a long drink from his water glass. "Sure."

We knew how this would go down. We weren't *part* of the Bible Belt, but we lived smack in the middle of it. These were good, God-fearing people who went to church both Sunday morning *and* Wednesday night and to Bible study in between. They drove home to fried chicken and collard greens and to *Thank You Jesus* signs staked into the red clay in their front yards.

And they prayed. *A lot.* In fact, someone stopped to pray for me nearly every week. I always thought that was weird—I mean, why me and not Hannah? Or Tucker? Now *there* was a kid who needed prayers. But it was always me. Sometimes they prayed for me to be freed of my terrible affliction, whatever that meant, but most times they didn't say what it was they were praying for. I kinda thought they might have been praying for happiness, because when they walked away, they always seemed relieved and happy.

It quickly became clear that this was not going to be that kind of praying.

There was a shrill scraping of metal on tile, and just like that I was face-to-face with the voice. He was a round man in a pea-green suit and a napkin tucked into his belt.

He didn't introduce himself or say anything at all. Instead, he drew a deep breath and rested his hand on my head. Mom and I cringed. He smelled of cigarettes and stale fried chicken.

As he exhaled he began to mumble softly. It was so quiet, I couldn't make out what he was saying. Bit by bit his voice grew until I realized he wasn't talking. He was chanting—*loud* chanting, like he wanted the whole world to hear. It was crazy, scattered noises and letters crammed together where they didn't belong.

Ambrazzzzishusss.

Franjooolico.

Whippo-whippo-whippo-que.

I already knew a lot about words, and I was sure these were made-up. Everyone else in Shoney's must have thought so too, because the clinking of silverware and buzz of conversation had stopped. Hannah and Tucker were frozen with their forks halfway to their mouths. Mom and Dad looked down, fingertips massaging their foreheads.

When the chanting finally ended, Mom swiveled in her seat until his hand fell from my head.

The man then raised his arms towards the fluorescent lights and said, "This child will have five gifts." He pulled the napkin from his belt and dabbed his forehead. "Give or take a few. I can't be absolutely sure of the number."

Awesome. My prophecy had a disclaimer.

The man sat back down at his table. The only sound in that Shoney's was the clinking of his fork against his plate.

Mom whispered to our waitress, "Check please."

Before we even left the Shoney's parking lot, I was obsessing.

Five gifts, more or less. More! Let it be more!

Maybe it was because my body was still missing, and I *needed* to believe. Or maybe it was that since I already knew two of my gifts, I *could* believe. Memory and words were great, but I wanted more.

Please, let it be more!

Tucker had found a plastic straw in his seat and was shooting spitballs at my sticker collection on the ceiling of the van. Normally, I would've flailed or screeched—these were *my* rewards from five years of doctors' visits—but right now, they didn't seem that important.

He took aim at one of my favorites—the Hulk, all flexed and muscly saying, "Your checkup was *grrrr*eat!"

Thwak! A spitball stuck to Hulk's nose, and Tucker pumped his fists.

"Maybe she'll have super strength like Hulk. No, wait! I bet she can fly! Wouldn't it be cool if she could fly? We can throw her off the couch and see if that's how you activate it."

Mom whipped around.

"We will not throw your sister off the couch to see if she can fly."

"I was just kidding," Tucker said. He shot another spitball.

"He didn't say she'd be a superhero, doofus," Hannah said. "Gifts don't mean superpowers. It's regular stuff. You know. Like singing or sports or . . ."

I didn't stick around to hear the rest of Hannah's regular stuff. I was cartwheeling down the beach. I was strumming my guitar. I was . . . what else?

Five gifts, more or less. More! Please let it be more!

CHAPTER 6
Age 5, The Year of the Buttered Cat

The next morning, Kali and Kasey came home, and Tucker told the whole story over breakfast. I listened, happy and full in my beanbag chair. This was how life was supposed to be. The five of us hanging out together in our kitchen.

"So who was this guy?" Kali asked.

Tucker shrugged. "Dunno. Some random dude at the restaurant." He kicked into a handstand and walked around the kitchen upside down for a few steps, then rolled onto his back. "Kinda smelled bad. And he looked like a pea or one of those olives from the salad bar."

Hannah turned the page of her book. "Oh please, if he were a vegetable, he would've been a lima bean."

We all cringed. There weren't many things that all five of us agreed on, but we all knew that eating lima beans was basically eating snot.

"Thanks for ruining breakfast," Kasey said, pushing away her cereal bowl.

"Oh, yeah, Mr. Bean! Crazy Mr. Bean." Tucker inhaled deeply then burped, "Misssterrr Beeeaaaannnn."

"Oh, grow up," Kali said. She straightened me in my bean-bag chair and brushed a curl from my face.

With her thick, dark hair and olive skin, Kali was an exact teenage version of me.

"So, what did you think of Mr. Bean and his five-gift prophecy? Did you believe it?"

I turned away. I wanted to believe it. But how crazy was it to get life-altering news from a lima-bean lunatic? Finally, I stuck out my tongue, just a little bit, and Kali understood.

"You kind of believe it."

I stuck out my tongue as far as I could.

"Then so do I," Kali said.

"Me too," said Kasey.

I smiled. They were in high school, so their opinions were legit. *Obviously.*

"Well, you already know about your memory. And there's your spelling and reading thing," Kasey said. She pushed her glasses up on her nose. "Do you want help finding the rest?"

Kali shook her head. "You can't help someone find their gifts. Self-discovery is done privately."

Hannah snorted and turned a page in her book. "A five-year-old's idea of self-discovery is figuring out who has the girl parts and who has the boy parts."

"Not Lexi," Kali said. "She's different. She understands stuff that even teenagers don't get."

"She was, like, *born* a teenager," Kasey said.

I sat up a little taller in my beanbag. I *was* advanced for my age, and having four older siblings made me seem even older.

Mom stuck her head in the kitchen. "I have a deadline this afternoon, so I need all of you to keep an eye on your sister."

Before anyone had a chance to protest, she disappeared down the hall.

"Well, it's been fun," Kasey said, standing up and stretching, "but I have to shower."

"Me too," said Kali.

Hannah slammed her book. "She said *all* of us. And if you leave, I'm telling."

"Fine," Kali said.

Kasey rolled her eyes but sat back down.

Tucker cartwheeled through the kitchen, into the den, and I guess onto the coffee table because there was a thud and a yelp. He hopped back into the kitchen on one foot. I laughed hard.

"Let's play hide-and-seek!" he said.

I stuck out my tongue.

"Are you sure?" Hannah asked. "You remember what happened last time?"

Did I *remember*? *Duh*. He hid me under a pile of dirty

clothes in his room and ditched me. The smell of sweaty gym socks burned into my memory.

But when Tucker promised to take me first *and* stay with me, Kali closed her eyes and started counting.

"I have an idea," Tucker said.

He carried me into the bathroom and towards the tub, which was half-filled with laundry.

I arched my back and growled. *Ggguuhhh.*

"They're clean."

True. The downstairs tub was cracked, so it was basically a holding tank for clean clothes.

He plopped me onto the pile, emptied another basket on top until I was buried, then dove in next to me just as Kali called, "Ready or not here I come!"

I gulped in deep breaths.

"Breathe softer or she's gonna hear us."

I heard tennis shoes and paws on the tile floor. The shower door swished open and shut.

"Whadaya think, Luke? Where are they?" Kali asked.

More footsteps. The closet door creaked, and I heard the squeak of metal hangers drug across clothing racks.

When that door closed, I sucked in one huge breath and held it until the footsteps faded—just long enough so Tucker would know we had fooled her.

Then I let out a burp, so loud that Luke woofed back.

Footsteps squeaked over the tile. Kali grabbed a handful of clothes, including the shirt Tucker was still wearing.

"Ouch!"

"You're it!"

"It's not fair! She gave us away on purpose."

Obviously. That was for the dirty gym socks.

Kasey and Hannah stood in the doorway.

"You're such a sore loser," Kasey said. "Just man up and start counting."

She positioned me on her hip and jogged down the hall. "Where to?"

I pointed to the closet.

We slipped inside. Kasey slumped to the floor and arranged me on her lap. It was full-on, middle-of-the-night dark. If there was one thing I hated, it was the disorientation of pitch dark. I flailed.

Kasey corralled my arms to my side. "You have to be still or they'll find us for sure. Take deep breaths."

I focused on breathing and stillness, but the harder I tried, the more I moved. My right foot flew out and banged the door. Kasey scooted backwards.

"Think of something else. How about your gifts? Pretty cool, huh?"

My body quieted as I stuck out my tongue to the pitch dark.

"You know two of them, but what about the rest? There's gotta be more. I bet this prophecy is a sign of good things to come."

I let that settle into my brain. *A sign. Of good things to come.*

It sounds so stupid now, but at the time, it all made perfect sense. It was time for my body to come in, and I needed to understand it when it finally got here. I needed operating instructions. That's where the gifts came in. *Obviously.* My gifts would be important—essential—for the life that was waiting for me.

The message from the universe was loud and clear: to get your body and your voice you need to find your gifts. From that moment on, my prophecy and my Epic Reasoning Fail became one hot tangled mess.

CHAPTER 7
Age 13, 21 hours until surgery

After twelve—count 'em, *twelve*—sticks, my IV is finally in place. I'm trying to stay calm, but my body hasn't gotten the memo. I'm hungry. I'm tired. My arm is throbbing.

My brain is obsessing about three things: eating breakfast, messaging with friends, and sinkholes. Yep, sinkholes. They've been on my mind a lot lately.

This spring, I was watching the news with Dad when up popped pictures of a massive sinkhole devouring a major road. In Charlotte. One moment you're driving down the street, minding your own business, then bam! You're plummeting into nothingness.

After that, I saw sinkholes everywhere. That crack in our driveway—was it just me or had it grown since yesterday? And that little hole in the backyard that I thought was a chipmunk burrow. Maybe it wasn't.

Then in the months leading up to this surgery, I realized I had my own personal sinkhole growing beneath me. Fear.

Fear of my upcoming surgery. Fear of the pain, and the risks, and that at the end of it all nothing would be better. And most of all, fear that this surgery would make things worse. By the time I could recognize these fears, I was hanging on with one hand, the rest of my body dangling into the nothingness of that hole.

Dad's phone pings. The Facebook ping.

Anna? Elle?

My arms flail. Gus hops back on the gurney, but Mom shoos him off.

"If you knock out her IV, I'm gonna lose my mind!"

Dad fishes his phone from his pocket and reads silently.

Really? I flail some more.

"Ken, please," Mom says, holding my arm.

"Okay, okay!" He clears his throat. "This one is from Adelle in London. 'Who wants this surgery, Lexi? You or your family?'"

"Me!" I'm so mad I have no problem belting it out, although out loud it sounds more like "Eeee!"

Dad sends my message, but he's shaking his head. "I wish we'd taken a picture of '*I am 13. Let me decide.*' Adelle doesn't know how pigheaded our girl can be."

I smack Dad's leg, but he isn't wrong.

With the first surgery, I was only seven, so Mom and Dad chose for me. They agonized over that decision.

That surgery turned out better than they feared but not as good as they hoped. Since then, I always got the feeling my parents had a tinge of regret. Like they had put me through a lot of pain, suffering, and worst of all, *expectation*, for a body that was a little calmer. That could puff out a few garbly words. Was it worth it?

When doctors here told us a second set of leads into another area of my brain could possibly help me even more, my parents got hung up on "possibly." They took me all the way to California so another *-ist* could tell me a second surgery was a crazy, fish-in-the-sky idea. Instead, she also said "possibly." When we returned home, I took the decision out of their hands.

I am 13. Let me decide.

I had spelled it out on my cookie sheet as Mom and I finished math homework. It had nothing to do with geometric proofs, but she understood.

Afterwards, there were still weeks of discussion and research, but in the end they did, in fact, let me decide.

Handing over that decision was the best gift my parents could have given me because it gave me control over my sinkhole, control over the fear that tried to swallow me whole. Or at least it did for a while.

A nurse opens my curtain wide. "The MRI is finally open. Let's get you in there while we can."

Gus stands at the curtain like a Walmart greeter. His entire back side is wagging as he welcomes the techs who have come to roll me down to the MRI.

"Lexi, your ADD service dog has completely forgotten his real job," Dad whispers to me. "He's my animal avatar."

I laugh. Dad has struggled with Attention Deficit Disorder his entire life, so he totally gets Gus. But "ADD service dog"? *Seriously confusing, Dad.*

Mom joins Gus at the curtain. As Walmart Greeter, she stinks.

"Before you start, make absolutely certain her stimulator is off. Also, make sure you draw any pre-op labs you might need while she's asleep. She's had enough pokes for the day."

Truth.

The techs roll me through the curtain. I feel a rumble beneath my feet, like my sinkhole is on the move again. This is not my first MRI here in Kansas City. I had one this spring when we came to make final decisions about surgery. That one didn't go exactly as planned. I thought I had dealt with all that, put it behind me, but right now, I'm not so sure.

I squeeze my imaginary rock. I turn it over in my palm and try to concentrate on the places where the edges poke into my skin. It's a little weird, but the pain is somehow comforting.

The soft whir of wheels whispers, *Hurry, hurry. Before it's too late.*

Deep breath in. My story. Breath out.

CHAPTER 8
Age 5, The Year of the Buttered Cat

As I sat in the pitch dark of that closet, I knew one thing for sure. I had to find my gifts. But how? I couldn't even get up off the floor by myself.

Hide-and-seek had fizzled so Kasey plopped me into my beanbag. "Okay, kiddo. Why don't you sit here and think about those gifts for a while?" she said.

Hannah picked up her book and sighed. "Go ahead. I'll watch her. But you *all* owe me."

Everyone scattered.

Luke collapsed at my feet. He rested his chin on my leg and looked up at me like, "Well? What are they?"

That's the problem, Luke. I have no idea.

I made a list in my head—*Gifts I Might Have*—but that went nowhere. Every gift I thought of was somehow related to the two I already knew. I was smart, but that had a lot to do with my memory. I was an expert at Hangman and Mad Libs, but that was because of my gift for words.

I squirmed and twisted. I wanted to get up and run away from it all. This was way harder than I thought it would be.

Hannah put down her book and smiled softly. "Wanna play Hangman or something?

I stuck out my tongue and squealed. Maybe using an old gift could help me find a new one.

She dragged me onto her lap and pulled over my cookie sheet. Of all the kids, Hannah was best at helping me spell. She knew how to hold my body and wrist just right.

"Okay, what's it gonna be?" She held up two fists. "Right for Mad Libs or left for Hangman."

I swatted left, but instead of hitting her fist, I sent the cookie sheet clattering to the floor. The noise must have startled Luke because he jumped up and yelped. The Cat, who had been staked out under a tent of old newspapers, bounded over and weaved in and out of Luke's legs, purring loudly. Luke ignored him.

"I don't know why we ever got you a cat," Hannah said with a sigh. "You don't appreciate pet ownership."

Luke stretched and fell back asleep, but The Cat stayed put. He pushed his paws back and forth on Luke's belly. Suddenly, Luke lurched forward and snapped. The Cat yowled and ran off.

"Mom!" Hannah shouted. "Luke just tried to eat The Cat!"

"I'm sure he didn't try to eat him. He probably just got fed up," Mom said, appearing in the doorway. She opened the back door and The Cat flew outside. She held up my shoes. "Anyway, we need to get to the grocery store if we want to eat tonight."

It rained every day for the next week. Other than therapy appointments, I stayed home because getting me in and out of the van in bad weather was a nightmare. My family seemed to have forgotten all about the prophecy. It didn't matter. Kali had said self-discovery was a private road trip, and that seemed about right.

Just *thinking* about gifts, however, had gone nowhere. I needed to get up, get out, and search. But how? I needed my body to find my gifts and my gifts to find my body.

On Saturday, the rain finally stopped, and sun peeked through the late afternoon clouds. Dad decided it was time to tackle a garage-swallowing junk pile. He hadn't been outside long when he shouted for us to come see what he'd found.

Kali, Kasey, and Mom, with me clinging like a koala bear to her hip, ran outside.

Dad pointed to a tarp-covered lump. "Guess what's under here!"

"Possum?" Kasey guessed.

Everyone stepped backwards.

Dad whisked away the tarp. "Voilà!"

It was a beat-up old stroller.

"That's it?" Kali asked.

Dad clasped his chest, pretending to be offended. "This is Lexi's new ride. Lexi, today you join a proud tradition of Haas children who have called this their first set of wheels."

"And only set of wheels," Kali mumbled.

"I don't know," Mom said. "I don't see how that could work for her."

"You worry too much," he said.

He kissed her cheek and pried me from her arms. He buckled me in and stuffed rolled-up towels around my head and hips to hold me in place.

"Pretty cool, Lex," Kasey said. "Are you ready to take her out for a spin?"

Out? Yes! That was exactly what my gift search needed.

I stuck out my tongue as far as I could, but when I did, my head jerked to the side. My face smooshed into the towel.

Mom sighed.

Dad jiggled my arms until my muscles relaxed.

"Don't worry, Mom," Kali said. She clipped Luke's leash to his collar. "We won't let all this luxury go to her head."

Dad called after us, "Take it nice and slow. It's a police magnet. Oh, and registration is in the glove compartment."

Kasey, Kali, and I turned off our quiet street and onto the main road, where cars zipped past rows of brick two-stories. The air was thick as syrup and steam rose from the pavement.

Sweat tickled my face and neck. I wanted to wipe it away, but when I tried to lift my arm, my entire body twisted. If my gifts were out *here*, I would never find them.

After a couple of blocks, Kasey wiped my forehead. "Maybe we need to go home and let Dad work on your new ride. You know, add a few more features."

Right then, a shirtless boy jogged past, sweat rolling down his tanned back.

Like I said, there have been times in my life when, out of the blue, words would just pop out of my mouth. I'd have a thought, same as always, but instead of getting stuck in my brain, the words would find a trap door or something and escape.

This was one of those times.

I took a deep breath and blurted, "Oh, yeah!"

My excitement was *actually* for rolling back to our air-conditioned house, but Kasey, Kali, and the boy didn't know that. He spun around to face us, jogging backwards for a few steps.

"Sorry!" Kali said. She pointed to me. "It was our little sister."

All eyes turned to me, so I did what any kid would do in

that situation. I pretended to be asleep. *Obviously*. Eyes closed, droopy head, and even a little drool dribbling from my mouth. From the corner of my eye, I saw the boy smile and give them a thumbs-up before he jogged off.

Kasey crossed her arms. "What the heck, Lexi? That kid is a lifeguard at the pool! Do you know what it's gonna be like next time we go? I'll tell you what. Awkward. *Super* Awkward."

"She can't help it," Kali said. "Sometimes her words just . . . happen."

"Yeah, and sometimes I'm not so sure."

I was suddenly so hot I thought I might explode into a fireball. I wanted to say I was sorry, but of course no words *ever* came when I wanted them to. All I could manage was *gg-guuhhh*.

Maybe words weren't my gift after all. What good were they if they were stuck in my head? Or hurled out randomly like a weapon?

I arched and groaned.

"Chill out, Lex. It's not so easy to be on the other side, either."

The other side? Since when were we choosing teams? If we were, I knew what they would be. Everybody who could walk, everybody who could talk, everybody who could *everything* on one side. Me on the other.

We walked home in silence. When we reached our drive-way, I could see Mom and Dad outside the garage. Their hands were flailing and gesturing. At first, I thought they were dancing. *Outside*. Where everyone could see them. That jolt of electricity that comes when parents do something embarrassing shot up from the base of my spine.

Kali's pace slowed. As we inched closer, I realized Mom and Dad weren't dancing. They were arguing.

The day's mail was scattered on the ground. Mom was waving a letter in hurricane circles. At the top, a fancy gold heading flashed with each turn of her hand.

"I don't see how this is going to fix anything, Ken. We've been down this road before. It's not going to work. It *can't* work. We have to focus on fixing it, not on getting even."

"*This* is not about getting even," Dad said pointing to the letter. "This is about what was stolen from Lexi. It's about the missing evidence."

"What missing evidence?" Kasey asked.

Mom and Dad jumped. Mom let out a long sigh and bent to pick up the mail.

"Oh, it's nothing," Dad said. He smiled. "You're back awfully fast. How was the walk?"

"Thanks to Lexi, we're gonna have to find a new place to swim," Kasey said.

Dad leaned on his broom. "Lex, did you use your super powers to blow up *another* pool? The neighborhood association's gonna be ticked."

"It's not funny, Dad," Kasey said. "When she learns to talk she's gonna be a nightmare."

Kali heaved me onto her hip. When she opened the back door, cold air rushed out. Luke bolted in.

I bent sideways in Kali's arms, hoping to get a glimpse of The Cat. I hadn't seen him since his run-in with Luke earlier that week, but no one else seemed to have noticed he was missing.

"What's wrong?" Kali asked.

I tried to make cat sounds.

"Sorry, kiddo. No idea. Try again?"

I breathed in deep. *"Cu. Cu."*

She frowned. "Maybe spell it out with Mom later? Oh, guess what? It's almost time for your favorite show!"

With her free hand, she dragged my beanbag to my TV-viewing spot and propped me up so I could see. I wasn't buying her distraction. I had spent enough time in this spot to know that if I arched hard enough, I had a direct view into the kitchen. If The Cat wasn't stalking Luke, he would be scouring the table for crumbs. In my enthusiasm, I threw my head back too hard and toppled to the floor.

Kali shook her head. "I don't get it. You love *Word Girl*. Look! She's flying over the city, ready to fight crime with . . . with vocabulary . . . and . . . stuff."

She sat me back up. I launched myself sideways again, this time on purpose.

How could I sit here and watch TV when so much was missing? Missing gifts. Missing evidence. And now a missing cat.

CHAPTER 9
Age 5, The Year of the Buttered Cat

I spent the rest of Saturday afternoon obsessing over all that was missing in my life. There was my body and my gifts, *obviously*, but according to Dad there was more. Lots more. Something stolen. Missing evidence. And that letter! Maybe whoever sent it could help me get everything back. But who was it? The fancy gold lettering looked official and important. Well, two things were for sure: 1) I had no way of getting my hands on it, and 2) Mom and Dad were *not* talking.

Sunday, our family gathered in the den for our weekly viewing of *Saturday Night Live*. Since the show started so late on Saturday, Dad always DVR'ed it. At exactly three o'clock Sunday, he would shout, "*SNL*," and like pigs called to dinner, everyone would drop what they were doing and shuffle to the TV.

"Lexi's the only five-year-old in America allowed to watch *SNL*," Kasey said as we settled in.

"That's because she's the only five-year-old who can understand it," said Dad, pushing buttons on the remote.

When the show flickered onto the screen, Dad pulled me onto his lap and folded my legs crisscross applesauce. He wrapped his arms tight around me. I always felt calm and steady when he held me this way. It was like he was my muscles. As he squeezed me, his breathing slowed to match mine, like I was his heart.

The *SNL* band started to play. Dad shifted me a little so I was facing the screen, but when the announcer said, "Ladies and gentlemen, Rainn Wilson," I slumped. I had seen this one last winter. Summer reruns were the pits when you could remember every single joke and skit.

Pretty soon, my thoughts drifted back to my missing things. I *had* to find them. All of them. By the first commercial break, I had settled on a plan. I would tackle my list from the bottom. Start easy and work up to the hard stuff.

After *SNL*, everyone scattered. Mom sat with me to spell. I pulled down letters until my cookie sheet read: **The Cat is gone**

She laughed. "That cat goes missing as often as my car keys. When he gets hungry enough, he'll be back."

But he didn't come back. A month passed with no sign of The Cat or my gifts.

Maybe The Cat would eventually turn up on his own, but I knew if I wanted to find my gifts, I would have to get up, get out, and search.

By September, I had hitched my hopes to one thing: MS. JOANN'S FRENCH FOR HOMESCHOOLERS.

The heading screamed in shimmery blue ink from a flyer stuck on our fridge door. Beneath the heading was a drawing of a little girl waving a French flag and under that, "Classes resume September 6. Your class is: Level 2."

"Level 2" was handwritten in red marker. At the bottom, the flyer read, "Please remember, do NOT park on my grass or my neighbor's grass!!"

I had started French with Ms. Joann the year before when my speech therapist told Mom a second language sometimes helps with "speech delays." Spoiler alert: it didn't work. But Mom thought it would do me good to hang out with other kids once a week, even if most of them were a year or two older than me. When the Level 2 info arrived, she signed me up again.

I had mixed feelings about it from the day the flyer appeared on the fridge. French was *okay*, and the kids were nice enough, but I had four friends at home. Why would I need more? But *now*, now that I was searching for gifts and evidence and maybe even more, I was actually looking forward to class.

The first day back, Mom parked at the bottom of Ms. Joann's driveway. As she unbuckled me from my car seat, she nodded to two boys poking sticks into a wide, muddy ditch.

"Avery. Marc. Excited for a new year?"

The boys shrugged. They didn't look up.

"I bet you'll learn loads this year," she continued.

I snorted. Mom gave me the stink eye, but she knew I wasn't wrong. These two hadn't turned in a single homework assignment last year.

Marc pulled his stick from the mud, examined it, and flicked it towards Avery. Red mud spattered Avery's jeans. Avery laughed and returned the favor.

"Well . . . see you in class," Mom said brightly, and we began our trek up Ms. Joann's long, hilly drive.

Halfway up, Mom stopped to catch her breath. "I think you gained a few pounds since spring. Either that or I'm getting old." She pointed towards the house. "Lexi, look!"

In the front yard, three girls stood hunched and gasping beside a ginormous tree. I smiled. They were McRae, Martine, and Martine's younger sister Alexa—three girls from Level 1.

Each had a hand or foot pressed against the tree trunk. Two other girls—one tall and dark, and the other tiny and blonde—raced towards them. The Trejos! It looked like all the girls from Level 1 were back!

"C'monc'monc'mon, Elleeeeee," McRae yelled, waving her free hand towards the dark-haired girl.

Elle planted a hand on the trunk just as the blonde girl made a swipe for her T-shirt. "Base!"

"Elle Trejo, I got you! I definitely got you!"

"Face it, Anna. Big sisters rule." Elle high-fived Martine.

Everyone laughed. I screeched and arched hard. Even *I* had forgotten how fun these girls could be.

The girls looked up.

"Lexi!" Anna cried.

They all raced down the hill and swarmed around us.

"Did you have a fun summer?" Elle asked.

Tongue out.

"Cool! Whadja do?"

I tried to answer, tried to tell them everything—the beach, the prophecy, the missing cat. I took a deep breath and arched my back, trying to shove the words out of my chest, but all I could manage was a little groan.

My indifference from last year came flooding back. Why bother making friends here when no one could understand me?

Mom wrestled me back onto her hip. She told them I had gone to therapy and hung out with my brother and sisters.

She's leaving out all the best parts.

Inside, parents chatted quietly. Older students recited French verb conjugations in the classroom near the kitchen. Ms. Trejo waved to Mom, and soon they were off in their own conversation. I twisted on Mom's hip to see the girls. They had circled up and were playing a clapping game.

"Miss Mary Mack, Mack, Mack all dressed in black, black, black," McRae sang quietly.

I watched their coordinated hand movements. *Cross chest, hit legs, clap middle.* Then it really heated up. *Hit the hand to your right, clap middle, hit a hand to your left, clap middle.*

Their bodies knew exactly what to do and when to do it. Most of these girls were a couple of years older than me. Maybe when I got to be their age my hands would do this too.

The girls clapped faster and faster until finally, McRae and Elle missed hands all together. I squealed, and Mom gave me a little squeeze.

"Do you wanna play, Lexi?" Anna whispered.

Ggguuhhh. Even my *eyes* couldn't keep up with their hand movements.

"C'mon," Anna said, pulling at my legs. "We can use your feet instead of your hands."

Without waiting for an answer, the five girls shifted over so that my dangling feet were within reach.

"My turn!" Elle said. She crossed her arms. "Ready? Miss Mary Mack, Mack, Mack all dressed in rainbow, rainbow, rainbow—"

Elle clapped my left shoe, but Anna stood with crossed arms.

"Elle! That's not how it goes, plus nothing rhymes with rainbow."

How about: That rule's a pain though, pain though, pain though.

"Does too." Elle held my hand as she spun around. "My sister's a pain though, pain though, pain though."

Did that just happen? Jinx! These girls get me!

Ms. Trejo shook her head and put a finger to her lips.

"You can say it however you want," Elle whispered.

The older students filed from the classroom.

"Au revoir, Madame Joann!"

"Bonne journée!"

As they crossed a red strip of tape at the classroom doorway, the conversation became, "Whatcha doing later?" and "Text me when you wanna do homework."

Our class lined up at the red tape. As we entered, Ms. Joann greeted each of us with *"Bonjour!"* and *"Comment allez-vous?"*

Mom started to take our usual seat in the back, but I flailed and pointed to the chair between Anna and Elle. Mom smiled and we moved up. This was where I wanted to sit every week. This was the spot for finding gifts.

Class began with a prayer in French. Ms. Joann, like everyone here except me and Mom, was part of the Bible belt, but her prayers were different from the random ones I got on the street. She prayed that we would all learn and love French language and culture, then she said a small prayer for each of us.

When it was my turn, she asked for my continued good health and happiness.

I wished she would add, *"S'il vous plaît, aidez Lexi à trouver ses cadeaux,"*—please help Lexi find her gifts—but she didn't.

After that, she told us to take out our *cahier de preparation,* or workbooks, and our new year officially began. Occasionally, Ms. Joann stopped to repeat something in English for emphasis, but otherwise everyone obeyed the French Only rule. When it was time to leave, my brain was thinking in French.

As soon as we were dismissed, everyone shoved their workbooks in their bags and tore through the kitchen shouting, "Race ya down the hill!" and "See ya at Bible study!"

"Au revoir, Lexi," Anna said.

Elle leaped over the red tape and shouted midair, "See ya outside, Lexi."

I pumped an arm and smiled.

On the way home I thought about Anna and Elle and the other kids. French was gonna be amazing this year. When I got my body, I would definitely learn how to play Miss Mary Mack.

As soon as I thought that, reality came flooding back. To get my body, I had to find my gifts. And to find my gifts, I had to *look* for them. I had been so distracted I hadn't even thought about them. Next week, I would do better. Next week, I would stay focused on what mattered.

CHAPTER 10
Age 13, 20 hours until surgery

I could not be an MRI tech for a bunch of reasons. For one, if I had to describe the procedure to my patient, it would go something like this:

The MRI machine is a gaping, metal beast. For fun, we've nicknamed him Thanos. Up front, Thanos has a long, padded tongue. Once you're asleep, we'll lay you on this tongue, and he'll slowly pull you into his mouth. The thing about Thanos is, he doesn't like you to move. You must be completely still. That's why we're putting you to sleep—so he can eat you in peace, without you thrashing around in there. Wait! Why are you banging on the exit door? Where do you think you're going?

Oh geez. I just realized there's another kid in here. From the look on her face, I think she read my mind. She looks terrified.

I'm sorry.

I smile at her and wave my hand, but my whole arm pumps up and down. I'm pretty sure I look like I'm conducting an orchestra. The kid doesn't seem to notice, or maybe she's just too scared to care.

I try to send her a telepathic message. *It's okay. These MRIs are really no biggie.*

Her eyes tear up. I've never really perfected that whole telepathy thing. What is she, seven? Maybe eight? Who sends an eight-year-old into this place alone?

Finally, I have no choice. I gulp huge amounts of air and let fly an impressively loud burp. She smiles through her tears. I smile back and try to make funny faces.

"You're shivering!" a nurse says to me. "Need a blanket?"

I nod and point to the kid, who's also trembling. The MRI room is always freezing, but I think her shivers aren't from the cold.

The nurse tucks several warm blankets around me, and it's like pajamas straight from the dryer. Just as she's wrapping a blanket around the kid's legs, an *-ist* walks in. My stomach lurches.

You can tell the *-ists* from the nurses and techs by the color of their surgical scrubs. This one is wearing a green cloth cap and face mask so he must have just come from the OR. He leans over my gurney. I squeeze my imaginary rock.

"Hi Lexi! Guess who?"

He pulls down his mask, and I laugh. It's Brian.

Steve Shapiro hired him last year to help run the neurosurgery program here. At first, he was Dr. Aalbers—just another -ist. But after a while, he grew on me. He's cool for a neurologist. Now, I don't demean him with the doctor title. He's been promoted to just plain Brian. He'll be in charge of programming my device, and he'll be with me in surgery tomorrow. *Thank God.*

"I have to switch off your stimulator before the MRI, but we're gonna knock you out at the same time so you won't be uncomfortable. I promise I'll turn it back on before you wake up. Okay?"

I stick out my tongue and laugh—gotta love an -ist who says, "knock you out" instead of something like, "proceed with sedation."

The first stimulator has calmed my body a lot, but it only works when it's on. If it's off, my body will squirm on this table like a bug on its back.

"Ready for tomorrow? And by *that* I mean ready for the really terrible haircut you're gonna get?" He picks up one of my braids. "You can kiss these goodbye."

Now I'm really laughing. He's not wrong. Surgeons can target tiny structures in the brain with sharpshooter accuracy, but they give lousy haircuts. The first couple of weeks are the worst. With two jagged incisions across my shaved head and wires bulging in my neck, I'll look like Frankenstein. People will gasp and grab their children when I roll by.

At first, I was a little worried about the haircut, but here's the thing. I didn't even have to tell Anna and Elle. They just knew. They threw a hat party with all my friends, and now I have like twenty hats, scarves, and bandannas. Good friends are just *like* that. They build a solid platform—no, wait . . . a *scaffolding*. (Thanks, Grade 5 vocab list. You came in handy after all). They build a scaffolding of steel and cement under your feet that props you up, so you don't fall into your sinkhole, so you don't give in to fear.

Suddenly, I'm serious again. *Anna, Elle, where are you guys? Please message me.*

Before I can obsess about that too much, there's a flurry of activity around my gurney. Someone turns on my IV, and I feel a cold rush in my hand. Brian holds a device called a programmer up to the place where the stimulator is implanted in my belly. The programmer magnetically changes the settings on the stimulator. Brian makes selections like he's making a withdrawal at an ATM.

"Unit is off," he says.

A second person looks over his shoulder and says, "Verifying unit is off."

There's no joking or messing around with this part. If I

went into the MRI with the stimulator still on, it could kill me. But this is Brian. Just. Plain. Brian. I am sure I . . . will . . . beeee . . .

CHAPTER 11
Age 5, The Year of the Buttered Cat

The day after French class was our first official day of home-school. Hannah, Tucker, and I were in the kitchen waiting for class to start at nine a.m., but Mom was nowhere to be seen.

"Mom's missing," Tucker announced. He spun upside down in his chair and hummed "The Star-Spangled Banner," loud and off-key.

I arched and groaned. I couldn't handle another missing thing in my life.

"Chill out, Lex. He's just kidding," Hannah said.

Finally, Mom shuffled into the kitchen, balancing her open laptop in one hand and a coffee mug in the other. Her cell was wedged between her ear and shoulder.

"So, I got this email from Lou Lattimore this morning," she said into her phone.

I didn't know who Lou Lattimore was, but Mom might as well have said she had gotten an email from the Dark Lord, because that's how grim her tone was.

There was talking on the other end that I could tell was Dad, but I couldn't make out what he was saying.

"Lou wants to dig a little deeper and needs our notes ASAP. You know how I feel about this, Ken."

There was more *blah, blah, blah* from Dad.

Mom sighed. "Okay, I'll get on it right away. But after this, I want as little to do with Lou as possible."

"Sorry guys," Mom said. She let her phone drop onto the kitchen table. "A little project has come up that I need to take care of this morning."

Hannah groaned.

"Okay, okay, how about this? The three of you work on something . . . maybe a poster or flyer about The Cat." She snapped her fingers and pointed to the family computer. "That's it. You guys make a missing cat flyer for English—"

"Mom!" Hannah shook her head.

"No? Okay. Then, recess. Make a missing cat flyer for *recess*. Print out a few, and after lunch we'll put them up around the neighborhood."

"Crushing it," Hannah called after her. "Crushing home-school!"

Mom waved a hand and turned towards her office. When she did, her laptop screen flashed towards me.

Tucker pumped his fists. "First day, free day!"

"Flyer. Now!" Hannah said, pointing to the computer.

She held me on her hip so I could see, but I wasn't thinking about the missing cat. It had only been a flash—a hot second, really—but I could've sworn that when Mom's laptop turned, I saw a fancy gold heading matching the one on the mystery letter. This Lou Lattimore guy was digging deeper into missing things. My missing things. Why didn't Mom want his help?

"Earth to Lexi!" Hannah said, giving me a little jiggle. "I *said*, what do you think of this?"

Tucker held my head steady, and Hannah ran her finger under each word to help my eyes follow:

MISSING CAT

Name: The Cat

Last seen: Not sure, but it's been a while

Appearance: gray fur, green eyes

If found: DO NOT APPROACH. The Cat should be considered armed and dangerous. Please call 704-333-2121

"Whadaya think? Hannah asked.

I gave an absentminded nod.

"You're right. It needs a picture." Hannah said.

Tucker scrolled through files of family photos, but there weren't many of The Cat.

Finally, a tiny thumbnail appeared in one corner. Tucker clicked on it, and the image filled the screen. It was The Cat perched near the top of our Christmas tree the year before, taken just before the tree fell over, smashing a dozen ornaments.

"Yep, that's the one," Hannah agreed. "If anyone finds him, they won't keep him long. He's kind of a jerk."

"He wouldn't let anyone bring him home," Tucker said. "He probably wouldn't let *us* bring him home."

He copied the picture under the Missing Cat heading, then stuffed paper into the printer.

After lunch, we loaded into the van, and Mom drove us around the neighborhood to post flyers on streetlamps and stop signs.

I was grateful for the uninterrupted time to think about Lou Lattimore. His name sounded like a superhero alias like Peter Parker or Bruce Banner. I pictured him flying over Charlotte in his cape searching for my missing things.

The van door slammed. I jumped.

Tucker wiped sweat from his forehead. "That's the last one. Now all we have to do is go home and wait for a phone call."

It would be a long wait.

CHAPTER 12
Age 5, The Year of the Buttered Cat

The day after our false start, school started back for real with Hannah and Tucker at the kitchen table and me in my bean-bag chair. Hannah worked on her laptop, wearing headphones to block out Tucker, who was once again upside down singing "The Star-Spangled Banner."

I was excited to be studying North Carolina history this year. On Thursday, Mom read me the story of Virginia Dare, the first English child born in the New World. Weeks after her birth, Virginia's grandfather, Governor White, returned to England for supplies. It took forever for him to get back to the colonies. First, he was stuck in a harbor with no wind, and when he finally got back to England, there was a war.

I held my breath as Mom read that when the Governor returned to North Carolina on Virginia's third birthday, he discovered that she and all the colonists had vanished. All he found was the word CROATOAN carved on a post.

"Not to interrupt or anything, Mom, but you *do* remember

that Lexi starts back to horseback riding today, right?" asked Hannah. She was standing in front of the refrigerator peeling an orange.

"Today? I thought that was next week."

Hannah nodded her head towards the calendar on the fridge. "Well, there's a big star on today's date that says Mitey Riders."

Mom looked at her watch. She jumped up, pulling on her shoes and my shoes. She swiped her car keys and purse from the counter, and we bolted for the door.

We only lived a few miles from Misty Meadows Farm, home to Mitey Riders Adaptive Horseback Riding. On the way, I couldn't stop thinking about Virginia Dare, separated by a whole wide ocean from people who loved her. It made me so sad and empty I wanted to go back in time and fix it. If Virginia had her own personal superhero like I did, he could fix it. Lou Lattimore could swoop down, grab Governor White, and fly him back across the Atlantic. The colonists would look up, and Virginia would look up, and there would be her grandfather, tucked under Lou's arm like a newspaper.

I sighed. *Impossible. They didn't have newspapers back then. Obviously.*

When we arrived at the farm, Mom signed me in at the barn office then carried me out to the loading area. Last year,

I had been the first rider of the day, but this year there was a new class before mine. The riding ring was humming with activity, and six empty wheelchairs sat waiting at the fence.

I watched as the horses were guided to a platform. The riders were lifted off and carried down a ramp. Their arms flailed, and their heads jerked as they were positioned in their wheelchairs. They looked like they were about Kali and Kasey's ages—teenagers—but why were they like this *now*?

Where are their bodies? Why haven't they come in?

A fear rippled through me. It had been nearly six weeks since the prophecy, and I had made exactly zero progress in my gift search. I hadn't considered the possibility of a deadline. What if there was one? What if I only had a certain amount of time to find my gifts before . . . before *this*? I watched as the kids rolled off in their chairs.

"Lexi, is that you?"

An old man jogged towards us. I arched my back and squealed.

He scooped me from Mom's arms.

"I missed you this summer. My farm is lonely without you." He gave me a big hug and kissed my forehead. "Lemme hear my name. I know it's in there. I know you can say it! Harry." He bounced me with each syllable.

I took a deep breath and puffed, "Hhh, Hhh."

"That's it. Ha-rry."

I looked into his eyes and saw the same ocean I had stared into with Dad. Deep, stormy blue. The keeper of a million secrets and promises and dreams. These eyes had watched kids learn to ride and then learn to walk. These eyes *knew* stuff. And they saw me walking and talking and riding my horse. All. By. Myself.

My body is coming. I'll find my gifts, and then my body will be here. I WILL.

"Let's get to the barn," Harry finally said. "Pepper is waiting."

After class, Mom signed me out in the barn office. I stared at a yellowing collage of photos on the wall. They all featured the same young woman on a prancing black horse. The horse was shiny and graceful, but it was his rider who stole the show. In every picture she had this smile—like she owned the place. Like she was doing what she was *born* to do.

I lunged toward her.

"What on earth are you doing?" Mom asked, reeling me back in.

I stared up at the wall.

"You like the pictures?"

Tongue out.

"That's Harry's wife, Marilyn. Look how young she was!"

She walked me around the room so I could see all the photos. "Marilyn used to compete in a type of horseback riding called saddle seat. Beautiful, isn't it?"

Saddle seat was obviously Marilyn's gift. Maybe I just needed to see a picture of myself with mine.

I imagined a frame and inside—*me*. I squinted and tried to see more. What was I doing in that picture? What was my gift that everyone would want to see up on a wall? But all I could see was me sitting in my beanbag chair against a white background.

I flipped around, burying my face in Mom's shoulder. She kissed the top of my head.

"We better get home and see what your brother is up to," she said, and she carried me back out in the sunshine.

CHAPTER 13
Age 13, 18 hours until surgery

I open one eye, and as soon as I do, Gus licks my face. My throat hurts, I'm thirsty, and I need to pee. I flail a little, and Mom leans over my gurney.

"Welcome back! You've been asleep for nearly two hours."

I motion towards my throat.

Mom guesses right and uses a straw to take juice from a cup to my mouth. Best. Juice. Ever. A few more sips and I feel my body springing back to life.

I'm kinda foggy about what happened after they turned on my IV. Once that stuff hits a vein, it works fast. Mom says anesthesia always makes me pass out quick and wake up slow.

When I finally woke up from my last MRI—the one this spring—the nurse was slapping my cheeks, and I think the janitor was vacuuming up for the night. I'm kidding about the janitor, but I really did find a cold washcloth on my forehead and a nurse patting my face. After that MRI, we hadn't even left the recovery room when Brian called Mom's cell and told us to come up to neurology as soon as we could. He had found something *unusual* on the images he wanted to show us.

The memory makes me shudder.

"Are you cold?" Mom asks.

Ggguuhhh. I don't want to think about that day right now. I open my mouth wide.

"Starving?"

Tongue out.

Trouble is, I have so many wires sticking out of me I look like the backside of a home entertainment center. I'm pretty sure I could pick up HBO and Cartoon Network with my setup.

The nurse peels the EKG stickers from my chest and back. She presses gauze on my hand. I grimace as she slips out the IV.

As Mom takes me to the restroom and changes me back into my clothes, Dad fills out hospital paperwork.

When Mom opens my curtain, I see the kid from the MRI. She's walking out holding the hand of someone I think must be her mom. She turns and gives me a little wave. I try for a thumb's up.

It's finally time to eat. In the hospital cafeteria Dad grabs two trays.

"Do you want pizza or chicken fingers?" Mom asks.

"Yeah!" I say.

"That's not a yes or no question."

"Yeah!"

She gets the message and puts both on the tray, along with milk, a cup of fruit, and chocolate cake.

In the checkout line, Gus has shifted back to Walmart greeter and catches the eye of the woman in front of us.

"You're very cute, but you're a service dog so I can't pet you," she says.

"Gus, you're working," says Dad.

Gus turns to Dad and smiles as if to say, "But look how cute I am!"

Dad makes him sit beside my chair. "Sorry. Her ADD service dog loves attention."

"Oh, interesting," the woman says. "I didn't know they had service dogs for ADD."

Dad smiles. "Yeah, I don't think they do."

At our table, Mom quickly cuts my food. She holds my head steady with one hand and shovels in lunch as fast as I can chew and swallow. She pours milk in my water bottle and squirts some in my mouth.

I can't use a straw—can't get the coordination to close my lips and suck up liquid. It's one of the things I hope to get from this surgery, because lip closure comes in super handy for talking.

And for not dribbling stuff down your front. Mom is mopping up the milk trickling down my chin. Her phone rings.

"Yes, this is Lexi's mom." She looks at Dad and mouths, "It's the lab," then says, "We're just finishing lunch in the cafeteria. Can you tell me which test needs repeating?" She sighs and shakes her head. "Okay, we'll be down shortly."

"Sorry, Lex, but we have to go to the lab. One test from this morning wasn't normal. They want to repeat it."

I groan. Another needle?

"Which one? What was wrong with it?" Dad asks.

He sounds concerned, which worries me. My right arm flails. Gus leans on it until it stops.

Please don't let it postpone surgery. I can't take another last day. The sinkhole beneath me grows. The scaffolding shakes, sending me skidding to the edge.

"They wouldn't tell me over the phone," Mom says.

"Want me to come too?" Dad asks.

Mom shakes her head. "Take Gus back to the house for some water and a rest, then we can meet up after."

My thoughts shift to the Ronald McDonald House and my sinkhole shrinks, just a tiny bit, but enough.

The house across the street is an amazing home base. After tomorrow, I'll be inpatient. I think the thing I'll miss the most about the outside world is the smell of fresh-made brownies as we roll in after a long day.

Dad and Gus walk with us until we reach the lab entrance. Before they leave, Gus jumps up and hits the handicap access button. As Mom rolls me inside, I hear Dad's phone ping—the Facebook message ping. This *has* to be them.

I screech, and everyone in the waiting room looks up.

Dad says, "Your message will be waiting for you when you get done."

I screech again. The lady behind the desk looks up and frowns.

"Don't worry. I won't read it without you," Dad says.

Mom signs us in, and we sit down. To wait. Again.

Deep breath in. My story. Breath out.

CHAPTER 14
Age 5, The Year of the Buttered Cat

Homeschool was now back in full swing. I was so busy with classes and homework I had no time to search for missing things. When we arrived at Ms. Joann's for my second French class, I promised myself that today there would be no fooling around. I would stay focused on finding my gifts.

The plan started smoothly. Mom remembered to sit between Anna and Elle. Before Ms. Joann said her prayer, I sent her telepathic messages asking her to pray for my gifts to show up. She didn't *technically* say that, but she did pray for my health, happiness, *and* knowledge, so I counted that as a win.

But after that, out of the blue, Ms. Joann announced she would be dividing us in *équipes* or teams. She pointed to me, Anna, and Elle and said, "*Équipe 1.*"

And just like that, my plan crashed. I had been included with the other kids. For the first time *ever*, I was part of a team. *Team 1*. My focus melted.

Ms. Joann made a T sign with her hands. "English."

The shuffling of book bags and shifting of chairs stopped.

"Today, your team will write and perform a skit for the class. We'll start outside—Avery sit down—and you may sit wherever you want, *other* than in the ditch."

Avery and Marc stopped high-fiving each other and slumped back into their chairs.

"You can work out your plan in English, but once you start writing, *everything* must be *en français. Comprenez-vous?*"

Everyone nodded.

"*Allez-y!*" She pointed towards the back door.

"Let's sit over there!" Anna said, pointing to the big oak tree in the front yard.

While Anna and Elle pulled out their notebooks, Mom arranged me on her lap.

"Can we write a play about our bunny?" Elle asked.

I stuck out my tongue.

"Yeah! He could be a magic bunny that talks!" Anna said.

"He talks in French, but only when you feed him carrots!" Elle shouted.

Watching them throw ideas back and forth was like watching them play Miss Mary Mack. I couldn't keep up. I wanted to tell them that the bunny should talk in French when he eats French green beans, but it was all moving so fast. My arms flailed.

Mom cleared her throat. "I think Lexi has an idea too."

"Oh, right! Sorry, Lexi," Elle said.

Mom took my cookie sheet from my bag. She brought it to every class, but I had never used it. Classroom discussions moved too fast.

As I dragged letters, Anna said, "That's cool, Lexi."

"Are you picking letters yourself?" Elle asked.

Mom nodded. "She's been spelling on this since she was a baby."

The girls watched until my board read **haricots verts** "*Haricot verts?*" Elle asked.

"I think she means the bunny should eat haricots verts," Mom said.

"French green beans to speak French! *Oui!*" Elle said. She took out her notebook and wrote:

<u>*Le Lapin Magique (The Magic Bunny)*</u>
Par Anna, Elle, et Lexi.

Below that, she wrote *Setting*.

"Any ideas?" she asked, tapping her notebook with her pen.

"Maybe it can be your house," Mom offered.

"*Non, non, non,*" Anna said, "*en français.*"

She was right. Now that we were moving on to writing, we had to speak French.

Mom took a deep breath. "Okay . . . *Les chevaux . . . doivent être à votre château?*"

Anna and Elle snorted. I bit my lip.

"What did I say?" Mom whispered.

Anna leaned over. "The horse should be at your castle."

Mom flushed.

"Do you want us to—"

"*Non, non,*" Mom said, holding up a finger. She cleared her throat. "*Le cornichon est au cours du lavage.*"

Anna and Elle rolled onto their backs. I shrieked so loud, Martine, Alexa, and McRae, who were sitting all the way on the porch steps, turned to look.

I didn't want to laugh. I mean, I knew how she felt, trying her best to be understood and getting it all wrong. But this was *so* wrong.

"Worse?" Mom guessed, her face scrunched.

Anna couldn't talk, but she nodded.

"The pickle . . ." Elle began. She wiped a tear from her cheek. "The pickle is in the wash."

We all lost it, including Mom.

"Mrs. Haas, no offense, but your French is terrible," Anna said.

"Anna!" Elle gasped.

"No, it's fine," Mom said. "It is."

"Maybe we should just talk directly with Lexi," Elle suggested. "We'll ask her questions, and you can just be her . . . *assistant*."

We all agreed. After that, our writing went smoothly. The girls asked me what color the bunny should be, and I spelled,

blanc et violet

A white and purple bunny was the most magical. *Obviously.* They asked more questions. When I flailed, Mom helped me spell out *my* questions. Elle wrote the whole skit in her notebook.

Just as we were finishing, Ms. Joann came striding up the hill, dragging two muddy boys behind her.

She pointed toward the house and called to the class, "*La maison.*"

The skits were fantastic! Martine, Alexa, and McRae were French poodles at a pet salon. Remy, Adam, and Trevor did one about a transformer named Pierre.

Finally, it was our turn.

Elle was narrator. She held her notebook and cleared her throat. "*Nous présentons 'Le Lapin Magique'.*"

She pointed to me, Anna, and Mom, who was holding me on the floor. I was the magic bunny, and in our opening scene, Anna was feeding me carrots. She made a little heart with her hands and said, "*J'aime mon lapin!*"

Since regular bunnies mostly just sit quietly and wiggle

their noses, I nailed it. But when Anna ran out of carrots and told the audience she would have to feed me *haricots verts*, I needed to speak. Thankfully, we had a plan.

As Anna fed me make-believe beans, Elle held up construction paper cut in the shape of a speech bubble. Inside she had written my line.

She pointed to the words, then to the class, and they all said together, "*Ces haricots verts sont fantastiques!*"

Then Anna pretend fainted. Everyone laughed. It was epic.

The speech bubbles were my idea, and they worked great. Our audience never missed a beat. At the end, Elle held up one last card: *La Fin*. Everyone clapped and cheered.

When the skits were done, Ms. Joann said, "*Fantastique! Au revoir, classe!*"

Everyone jumped from their seats and bolted for the door, nearly knocking over Ms. Trejo, who was headed in to help clean up. I watched Anna and Elle through the window as they ran down the hill.

Mom held me with one hand and stuffed my workbooks into my book bag with her other hand.

Ms. Joann squeezed Mom's arm. "Great job today, but are you okay? I'm sure sitting on the floor with her isn't easy."

Non! En français! Ms. Joann had broken her own rule! I jumped hard at the breach.

I don't remember falling or hearing the thud as my head

hit the floor. When the room came back into focus, I had a bag of frozen peas on my forehead. Ms. Joann and Ms. Trejo were both kneeling beside me.

Mom was cradling me with shaky hands. "I can't believe I dropped her."

She peeked under the peas and winced.

Ms. Trejo patted Mom's shoulder. "It's just a bruise. I'm sure she'll be fine."

Tears blossomed in the corners of Mom's eyes. She tried to blot them, but they poured over her fingers and onto my shoulder. I arched, but she held me tighter. I could feel her heart pounding. *Why?* She had seen worse. Tucker split open a body part nearly every week. If this was just a bruise, why was she so upset?

I arched harder. Mom took in a deep breath like she was trying to suck all that emotion right back up through her nose and into her belly. She struggled to her feet.

"Maybe you should go to the ER or urgent care, just to be on the safe side," Ms. Joann said, walking us to the door.

Mom shook her head and squeezed me tighter.

"I know it's hard, but maybe you should consider getting her a wheel—"

"Thanks so much for class today," Mom interrupted. "I'll let you know if we have questions about homework."

That night, I lay awake in bed, my forehead pulsing with my heartbeat. I could hear the low hum of my parents' conversation on the other side of the wall.

As I focused in, Mom's voice became clear. "You were right. Lexi was robbed. We were *all* robbed. We have to try to get some of it back."

"Yes! Exactly!" It was Dad, although his voice was higher pitched than usual. "Lou Lattimore can help. If you'll just wait for—"

"I'm not waiting for someone to swoop in and save the day, Ken. This is real life. *Her* life. I need to do this."

There was a long silence. Finally, Dad sighed. "Go ahead. Do your research. But we can't get it back, Susan. It's gone. We need to move forward. It's what's best for her. It's what's best for all of us."

The conversation stopped. I let out my breath, long and slow.

Robbed? When were we—when was *I*—robbed?

There was so much missing. My body. My gifts. Even The Cat. What had the thief taken? Whatever it was, Lou Lattimore, real life superhero, was on the case. Lou was gonna try and get it back. Unless Mom beat him to it.

This was spinning out of control. I had to find out what had been stolen.

CHAPTER 15
Age 5, The Year of the Buttered Cat

The day after my fall, Mom was in a terrible mood. She snapped at Tucker for not sitting upright in his chair and brushed off Hannah when she asked for algebra advice. Instead of working with me, she plunked me on my beanbag in front of a DVD and disappeared into her office.

When Hannah finished her math, she asked if I wanted to spell with her. I stuck out my tongue.

"Mad Libs or Hangman?" she asked.

Ggguuhhh.

"Do you have something you want to say?"

Tongue out.

She pulled over my cookie sheet.

I wrote: **When were we robbed**

"What do you mean? We've never been robbed."

Ggguuhhh!

I pulled down three more letters: **SHH**

"Did you just shush me?"

Tongue out. If Mom heard us, she would know I had been eavesdropping and that would be the end of my main source of information in this house.

I spelled, **I heard Mom say it**

"No, you didn't."

I rapped the words with my fist.

"Maybe you misheard her. You *do* mishear sometimes."

Ggguuhhh.

I dragged more letters. **What about The Cat**

Hannah laughed. "What about him? If anyone stole him they'd bring him right back and probably throw in flowers and a sympathy card."

I glared at her. She was about as useful as a paper pool float.

"If you really want to know, you should ask Mom yourself. Now Mad Libs or Hangman?"

I did not ask. There was no way I was giving up my information source that easily.

A month passed.

French class was turning out to be loads of fun. Mom always sat between Anna and Elle, which meant Ms. Joann usually teamed us up for class activities. Mom always brought my cookie sheet, so the girls asked *me* the questions.

The rest of my life wasn't going nearly as well. My gift

quest had stalled. On top of that, The Cat was still missing. Occasionally, my sisters loaded me in my stroller and searched the neighborhood, but no cat or gifts came of it.

There was also no more talk of the robbery or Lou Lattimore. Well, at least no *overheard* talk. Every night, I settled my breathing and stared at my wall. If magic turned out to be one of my gifts, I'd make that wall melt like warm chocolate. Or I'd get Extendable Ears from the Weasleys' joke shop in Diagon Alley. Eavesdropping would be a breeze with those.

As it was, all I overheard were Dad's tunes and an ongoing debate about "supportive seating."

Dad said I needed a chair where I could see the world. Mom said I could see the world fine from her arms.

Dad said it was just a chair. That had wheels. No big deal.

Mom sobbed. It was a *wheelchair*.

There was a nightly discussion. I was on Dad's side. Mom was being dramatic. What was the big deal about getting me a rolling chair?

Dad finally won. An equipment guy came to therapy, and I lay on the floor while he and my physical therapist, Gail, measured my legs, then torso, then hips.

I watched Mom watching us. She paced. Her arms crossed, then uncrossed. She shoved her hands in her pockets then pulled them out. She smoothed her hair. It was like her empty arms had no idea what they were supposed to do *now*.

I tried telepathic communication: *Once my body comes in, we can give the chair away. Or use it as a coat rack. Or Tucker can have it next time he breaks a bone.*

When they were done, Gail held up a brochure and told me I could pick any color frame.

Any color?

I squealed and Mom finally smiled.

The wheelchair arrived on a Friday afternoon in October. My entire family swarmed around the delivery van like they were greeting a new pet. The equipment guy unloaded the chair onto the driveway. Everyone oohed and aahed over the sparkly blue paint that looked just like a summer night sky, and my name stitched on the seat in cursive, pink lettering. Dad loaded me up and took my picture, then Tucker ran with me up and down our driveway.

"You'll be able to see everything in this!" Kali said.

Mom was sitting on the front porch holding her knees. Dad sat down and hugged her.

"I have an idea!" Dad said. "The Renaissance Fair is in town. Why don't we go tomorrow so Lexi can try out her new chair?"

Mom shrugged.

"I think I saw a coupon for tickets online. C'mon! It'll be fun!"

"It does sound fun," Mom said, but her voice didn't sound like fun at all.

Tucker rolled me to the porch.

It's just for a little while. Just until my body comes in.

Mom didn't look up. Maybe telepathic messages only went through when the sender had complete confidence in their message. I tried again.

It's just until my body comes in. My body is coming! I just need to find a few more gifts.

Mom slumped over, her head in her hands, and I thought she looked like Governor White returning to Roanoke Island to find his colony gone. His family gone.

CHAPTER 16
Age 13, 16 hours until surgery

I'm in the blood draw room in the lab. My arm is out, my head is turned, and I'm trying hard to control my breathing. But the needle isn't the biggest pain in here.

Across the hall a boy is screaming, "Don't poke me, don't poke me!"

I feel for the kid—I really do. *He* is not the pain. It's his mom, whose sobs are drowning out her kid and for sure flooding the whole hospital.

"I'm so sorry, baby boy! I don't want them to do this to you either, sweet baby!"

Okay, Pro Tip: if you need a blood test and your mom is gonna act like this, send her out for ice cream. Or at least close the door.

"All done," my tech says, pressing a pink Band-Aid on my arm and tugging off her gloves.

It was my electrolyte balance that had been off in the first test, probably because I hadn't eaten or drunk anything. Now, since I just had lunch, my veins are nice and fat.

The tech shouts—so we can hear over the horror show across the hall—that my electrolytes are now back to normal.

It's time to bust outta here.

We roll out into the warm Kansas City sun and past the playground. For a hot second, I want Mom to carry me up the slide and let me pretend I'm a little kid again. But I see a man and a dog walking toward us in the distance.

Dad and Gus both give me a kiss, and I wait for Mom to fill him in on the lab visit. When they're done, I point to his pocket.

"I didn't read it yet, just like I promised."

I want to say, "Start!" or "Read!" but I've never been good at *s* or *r*. Instead I say "Go!" and he gets it.

He pulls out his phone. My arms flail.

"This one's from Betty in Charlotte."

My arms go limp.

"She says, 'I'll be praying you don't get an infection. My son had surgery once, and he got a bad one. Took a year to get over it.'"

Seriously, Betty?

"Lexi, you know don't have to respond to every message, right?" says Mom.

I stick out my tongue. I don't know what I would say to this one. *I'm sorry your kid suffered through that? I'm sorry that you suffer from such lousy timing?* I think I'll just leave it, but now, my brain is stuck on *infection.*

It's a big deal, for sure. You can minimize the risk, but it will never be zero. It happens, even in the best hospitals. And if I'm one of the unlucky people who gets one, it means that all the wires, electrodes, and stimulators will have to be removed. Everything from both surgeries. I would be back at square one.

It's a huge gamble, but we've done our homework. Tucker found a way to pull records online to compare infection rates for hospitals and procedures across the country. This place had one of the lowest rates anywhere.

Mom is looking at me with her head kinda tilted to one side. I'm sure she knows I'm obsessing. She pats my legs.

"Guess what? We have the rest of the afternoon off. Where would you like to go?"

I uncurl a finger and point to a limestone column that towers over the skyline—the Liberty Memorial.

"Go."

We roll toward the street, and I sink down in my wheelchair.

Deep breath in. My story. Breath out.

CHAPTER 17
Age 5, The Year of the Buttered Cat

The morning after my new chair arrived, Dad loaded it in the back of the van, and we headed off to the fair. No one had much to say during the ride except the wheelchair, which thumped and squeaked every time we drove over a bump.

Finally, we pulled into a grassy field that was the fairground parking lot. Dad asked a guy in an orange vest if there was accessible parking. The man pointed toward the fair entrance.

We pulled into a spot up front, and Dad hung a new blue-and-white placard in the rearview mirror.

"Dad!" Kasey gasped. "We can't park here! This is for *handicapped* people."

Mom pulled her sunglasses over her eyes and unbuckled my car seat.

"Mom!" Kali said. "We can't . . ."

Dad swiveled to face us. His eyes were filled with unfamiliar harshness. "Drop it."

Why was everyone so bananas over this whole chair deal?

It's just until my body comes in. Geez, people, chill.

We entered the fair through what looked like the walls of a castle. Kali had been right. I could see loads from my new seat.

I craned my neck, trying to take in everything at once. A row of shops peddled all sorts of "Ye Olde" stuff—Ye Olde candles, Ye Olde jewelry, Ye Olde pizza.

Jugglers and magicians worked the crowd for tips, and a fortune-teller chanted from behind wispy, red curtains.

My eyes finally settled on a large blonde woman who was trying to draw someone—*anyone*—into conversation. She wore a long, maroon gown that swooshed when she walked. Her top was laced so tightly that—as Kasey pointed out with a snicker—her boobs hovered right under her chin like two fat sidekicks.

Kali laughed. "She's an actress playing the role of a wench. But not very well."

"Excuse me. Haveth you the time," the wench shouted as a couple walked by.

The couple didn't look up.

She swished side to side, scanning the crowd.

"Look away or you'll be sorry," Kali warned me, but it was too late.

The wench sashayed over and posed in front of me with her arms stretched wide. I now had a clear view of her sidekicks.

They looked like they were strapped in with a tiny piece of white fabric and some leather lacing.

"Well, hellooo there youngeth one."

"Told you so," Kali whispered.

"I knoweth a secret! Can I telleth you? Can you keepeth a secret?"

Without waiting for an answer, the wench bent over my chair.

Then three things happened at once: 1) my brother and sisters ducked, like you do when you see someone about to get hit with a pie; 2) my parents lunged forward and tried to stop the inevitable; 3) my arms flew out, and the fingers of my left hand became tangled in the leather lacing that was holding up the sidekicks.

The entire event was over in seconds, but even now, years later, the replay in my head is in super slo-mo. I tugged and writhed while the wench struggled to free herself. My parents stood by helplessly, knowing there was no way they could reach in *there*.

In the end, my hand won, flying free while still clutching the fabric and lacing. The two sidekicks saw their chance and made a run for it.

I don't know what happened to the wench after that. Mom grabbed my arm, which was waving the fabric and lacing like a victory flag.

Dad wheeled me away, dragging Tucker behind us as he protested, "But I wasn't done here yet!"

The rest of the afternoon was a regular day at the fair. Kali and Kasey browsed Ye Olde shops while Tucker and Hannah played games. Dad held me on a merry-go-round powered by five hulky guys.

Late afternoon, as we rolled toward the exit, a jester jumped in front of my chair, blocking our path. He was dressed head to toe in green and wore pointy shoes with bells on the toes. He didn't speak but waved a fat, gold coin in my face. With an exaggerated twist of his arm he fanned out his fingers to show they were now empty. Then he reached behind my ear and pulled out the coin.

I yawned and stared past him toward the parking lot.

The jester turned to my family. "I just blew her little mind!"

Suddenly, I was wide awake, gulping in deep breaths. *No. You. Did. Not!* I wanted to belt it out, word by word. Instead, I lost it.

I held my breath, kicked my legs, and flailed my arms. In a flash, my family surrounded me.

Hannah leaned over and whispered in my ear, "Don't worry Lexi. He's the one with the little mind."

A girl walked by, holding a lady's hand. She twisted around to look at me.

"That girl in the wheelchair—what's wrong with her?" she asked.

"Well, Lydia, it looks like she's upset," the lady said. "I'm sure she'll be okay."

"No! I mean why is she like *that*? What happened to her?"

I stopped holding my breath. My arms and legs flopped.

"Why is she like that? What happened to her?" What does that mean?

We hurried out of the fair, and Mom lifted me into my car seat. She wiped my sweaty, dirt-streaked face and kissed my forehead.

I pretended to sleep all the way home, but my mind was racing.

"Why is she like that? What happened to her?" Where is my body? Where are my gifts?

CHAPTER 18
Age 5, The Year of the Buttered Cat

The week following the Renaissance Fair dragged by. Even school felt hard. I struggled with questions, new and old. *What happened to me? Why am I like this? When will I find my gifts so I can get my body?*

One thing was for sure. If Lou was out there looking for my missing things, he needed to step it up.

On Thursday morning, Mom drove me to the farm for horseback riding. She loaded me in my chair and wheeled me to the barn. At the dismount area, six empty wheelchairs sat waiting. The teams had been out on the trail, and I could see them trudging back up the hill. The riders slumped in their saddles.

I scanned the empty chairs. These weren't tiny or sparkly blue like the night sky. They didn't say *Lexi* in pink cursive on the back. But other than that, these wheelchairs looked exactly like mine.

I screeched and flailed. Mom inspected me, like she might see a bee fly from my shirt and a welt appear. When she couldn't find an obvious explanation, she rolled me to a quiet area away from the barn.

"What's up with you, Lexi? You've been off all week."

I wouldn't look at her.

"Don't you want to ride today?"

Ggguuhhh.

"But you love riding. I don't get it."

Harry came over and tried to make me laugh, but I wouldn't look at him either.

"Maybe she's coming down with something," he said. "Take her home and let her rest. We'll ride next week."

On the drive home, I thought about my wheelchair and *those* wheelchairs.

It's not the same. My body is coming in. Soon. Please let it be soon!

I leaned hard in my car seat and scanned the sky. *Please hurry, Lou, please.*

To this day, I can't remember what happened over the next month. Crazy, right? Me, the girl who remembers everything. I know by the calendar that we had Halloween, and I guess I went trick-or-treating, although I don't know what costume I wore. I don't know if anyone called about The Cat, or what we studied in French. On any given day, I couldn't even tell you what day it was. Tuesday? Friday? *Whatever.*

My attention had taken a detour as the new questions took over. *What happened to me? Why am I like this?*

I was tempted to ask Mom during my spelling sessions, but I could never get up the nerve. What would I say? What if she told me, and it was really, truly horrible? Could I handle that? After all, once I knew, I could never unknow it.

One morning, I was sitting on my beanbag, half watching Mom work with Tucker. She had a gauze bandage on her wrist, and Tucker seemed more interested in how she burned herself than in his spelling list.

A faint cry came from the back porch. Luke sat up and barked.

Tucker ran to the back door, and a gray streak flew inside.

The Cat figure-eighted Luke's legs, purring loudly. Luke lay down and licked his cat with the passion of a kid who had been handed a ginormous ice cream. The Cat was thinner and covered head to toe in a greasy film, but other than that he seemed healthy.

It only took a minute for the smell to fill the room.

Hannah pinched her nose. "What's he gotten into?"

Tucker pulled his shirt up over his nose. "It smells like . . . like buttered cat."

I've heard that our sense of smell is closely linked to memory. If we smell something distinctive and familiar it can transport us to another time. I guess that's what happened because, suddenly, I was watching Luke push away butter wrappers and vegetable peelings to reveal a tiny, gray kitten. The air had the fresh warmth of early spring. Mom was wearing old pink running shoes. Tucker was laughing and jumping up and down.

I could see it all. Every. Single. Detail. Like it was happening at that very moment. It was no longer a fake memory. This was the real one.

"What crazy, perverted person woulda buttered The Cat?" Tucker asked.

"He probably just got into someone's trash because he was hungry," said Mom. "Luke doesn't seem to mind."

That was an understatement. The two lovebirds spent a cozy afternoon curled in the den. Luke cleaned every inch of The Cat's little buttered body for the second time.

The smell lingered in the house and in my memory. As the afternoon wore on, I developed a plan. Before, I thought my complete set of memories began when I was two, but the buttered cat memory suggested they were all there. I just had to figure out how to get to them—at least some of them—and then I could connect the dots of my past. Maybe, just maybe, knowing my past would solve the mystery of my missing body.

If memory really is your gift, then use it. Obviously.

But knowing my memories were there and finding them

were two very different things. Familiar odors might bring them on, but that wasn't practical or reliable. Instead, I waited until nighttime, when I'd lie in bed with my mind completely free. I closed my eyes and thought back as far as I could, then tried to push further. I worked off bits and pieces, emotions, smells, and sound bites. Slowly, over several weeks, I saw slivers of my past, but nothing connected them. I revisited them over and over anyway, hoping they would eventually fit together like shards from a shattered mirror.

The first memory was of me sitting in Mom's lap as she worked at her computer in the middle of the night. The soft, blue glow of the screen created an island of light around us. The house was dead quiet except for the *clickety-clack* of her keyboard. She would type, stare at the screen, then stop and rock me back and forth. Type, stare, rock.

I soon realized this wasn't a memory from a single night or even a single house. Some of them were from our house in Virginia, where I was born, and some were of our house in Chapel Hill, where we lived when I was a baby.

I've been told that I didn't sleep for more than a couple of hours at a time until I was two years old, so I guessed that these were memories of Mom working through the night, trying to keep me quiet so I didn't wake everyone. In some of these memories, I was on Mom's lap and in others I was on her shoulder or in a baby sling. But always there was the *clickety-clack, clickety-clack, stare, rock, rock. Clickety-clack, clickety-clack, stare, rock, rock.*

Next was a daytime memory. Mom was holding me in a front pack, face out so I could see. Tucker was clinging to her leg. We were standing in our driveway in Virginia. A man in a grease-stained jumpsuit was loading our car onto the back of a flatbed truck. Mom was trying hard to smile, but I could see she was crying a little. Our neighbor leaned on the wood fence and asked if we were okay. Mom waved and told him we were fine.

After that, Mom was carrying me in the front pack through our empty house. All the furniture was gone, all the mess and the chaos were gone, and it was just emptiness. Emptiness that echoed with every footstep. Had we been robbed? Was this the theft?

Mom slammed the door behind us hard, and it rang out with her frustration. She ran with me fast down the hill and into the field where our swing set stood, also empty.

Then Mom did something weird for someone who had just been robbed. She sat down with me on a swing and pumped her arms and legs. We swung higher and higher until I could see past our garden and field, over the trees, and to the mountains in the distance.

The last memory was again a series, probably four or five. In each, I was naked on a table in a doctor's office, only it was never the same table or the same doctor. But they all did the same things. They moved a finger or a pen back and forth in front of my eyes and shone a light in them. They held me in their arms and tickled my spine and feet. They asked Mom questions.

Lots of questions. Until I fell asleep.

CHAPTER 19
Age 13, 15½ hours until surgery

The National World War I Museum and Memorial sits high on a hill overlooking Kansas City. It's one of my favorite places. In front, there's a long, flat lawn with the Liberty Memorial rising from one end like a limestone exclamation mark. It reminds me of the mall in Washington, DC. Beyond the monument, there's an overlook with an amazing view. I point to that when we arrive at the park.

We roll from the lawn, past the Liberty Memorial, and up to the courtyard wall. Mom stands me up to see the skyline.

It's weird, but there's something about this view that makes me feel grounded, rooted to the earth. I think it's because here, you see not only the whole city, but the wholeness of the city.

Just below us is one-hundred-year-old Union Station, with ginormous arched windows and crisscrossing train tracks. In the distance is the modern, curvy Kauffman Center for the Performing Arts. There are other icons too, and you can see them all from right here. But life in this city is more than icons. Neighborhoods, schools, and parks are wedged in too, and those little slices of ordinary are what I love. In those little pockets, lives roll along, unaware of me, my problems, my drama. I lean against the wall and soak up all that ordinary, and my mind settles.

The first time Mom brought me up here was this past spring, after Brian called us into his office to show me my MRI. That day, he pulled up pictures of my brain on his computer. He pointed out different areas with his pen, like a tour guide at a museum. The brain part looked like cauliflower or a half a walnut, depending on the view, but in all the pictures, the wires from the first surgery stood out like two glow-in-the-dark snakes.

Finally, Brian rested his pen on a tiny dark spot near one of the wires.

"I'm guessing no one has noticed this spot before, probably because it didn't cause any real damage," he said. "It had to have happened when her first leads were placed."

"Wait! Back up," Mom said. "What is that? What happened?"

Brian looked up from the computer. "This spot is a brain lesion. These pictures suggest that during her first surgery six years ago, Lexi had a stroke."

With that memory I arch hard, and I'm brought back to the courtyard. Mom struggles to keep me upright. Dad grabs my arm, and they guide me back into my chair. The wind whips over me, and even in the July sun, I shiver.

We roll down the path to the front of the museum, where a massive frieze overlooks two fountains and the sloping North Lawn.

"'These have dared bear the torches of sacrifice and service . . .'" Dad reads, but my mind wanders back to that spring afternoon in Brian's office.

The stroke had been minor, he told us, and didn't do any serious damage—at least not to my brain.

It did a number to my psyche. It opened that sinkhole beneath my feet. It was the beginning of my fear. After all, that first surgery when I was seven had been at a first-rate hospital. The surgeon was world-renowned. The surgical team was thorough and careful. None of that mattered. I still had a stroke.

Bad things only happen with bad doctors in sloppy hospitals, right? Right? The question echoed in that sinkhole as I slipped closer to the edge.

I asked Mom to tell me about strokes. She told me that mine was a fluke and was unlikely to happen again. She warned me that reading about them might make me feel worse instead of better. I didn't care. I wanted to shine a flashlight down my sinkhole.

She read me information from the internet. I learned that strokes happen when the supply of blood to the brain is interrupted. There are a couple of kinds: the kind older people get and the kind unlucky people get. Mine was the unlucky kind.

"Severe strokes kill, but even minor ones can cause lasting problems. They can cause difficulties with balance and speech," Mom read.

Ha! I get the last laugh there!

"If the stroke occurs in the temporal lobe, the patient can experience memory loss, which can be severe and permanent."

Memory loss? Severe and permanent?

I pointed frantically to my spelling board. Mom held my wrist, and I wrote: **Temporal lobe. Show me!**

She pulled up a diagram of a brain on her computer and focused in on a blob at the bottom of the skull. It looked like a wad of discarded gum.

My eyes flickered over the blob. I willed them to focus on the structures inside.

The labels! Go to the labels, I commanded them.

Hippocampus, I read. My eyes broke free and darted to the left.

I corralled them back. *Amygdala.*

They tried to dart off again, but I locked them down and focused on an egg-shaped structure near the top of the temporal lobe. The word came into focus.

Thalamus. The exact destination for the ice fishing contest my brain would be hosting a few months later.

When I read that, I toppled into the sinkhole, barely grasping the edge.

I was okay with the risk of gaining little—even nothing—from this surgery. I was even okay with losing skills I had never mastered. But losing my memory?

My breathing was ragged and shallow. How can the universe be that . . . that *unfair*? I had already lost so much. I had fought back despite the heartache. And this, *this* was my consolation? Was it a dealbreaker?

Nearly every day since, I've asked myself that question. *Is it a dealbreaker?* Each day, a new answer. Some days I'm strong and ready to charge into the future. Other days, I remember my first ever glimpse of the Atlantic, or the thrill of hide-and-seek, or Anna pressing that rock into my hand. And maybe worst of all, I think of my story, my evidence. Then I am weak.

I haven't told my parents about my second thoughts because if they knew, it would be over. They would feed into my worries. Even though they would say it was up to me, my decision could never be completely independent of their fears.

The wind gusts, misting us with water from the fountain. Gus jumps in and out of the spray like a little kid in a lawn sprinkler. Mom laughs, and we roll back up the path toward the museum entrance.

We stop for a moment at the Walk of Honor, a path of granite bricks bearing the names of servicemen and women.

An old man in a faded army cap is placing carnations on some of the bricks. When we roll past, he puts a red carnation on my lap. I extend a shaky hand and attempt a salute. He extends a shaky hand and salutes back.

I take in a deep breath. My story. Breath out.

CHAPTER 20
Age 5, The Year of the Buttered Cat

For the next several weeks, a battle raged in my brain. On one side were the fragmented memories of my past and the questions from the Renaissance Festival. *Why is she like that? What happened to her?*

On the other side was my Epic Reasoning Fail. It had strong roots, and it wasn't going down without a fight. My body was still coming. It *was*.

The holiday season came and with it, a ceasefire. Thoughts of missing things, the robbery, and my past were shoved aside for tree decorating, Christmas carols, and most of all, the promise of Santa.

A few days before Christmas, when I sat on Mom's lap to spell, she had a surprise.

"Today, we're going write a letter to Santa and deliver it to him at the mall. That way, when he asks what you want for Christmas, you'll be ready. You can spell it on your board, then I'll write it on this."

She held up a piece of stationary with a border of holly and Christmas gifts.

"Do you know what you want Santa to bring?"

Ggguuhhh.

"Do you want a minute to think about it?"

Tongue out.

"Lexi!" Tucker called from the kitchen. "Santa in his sleigh, Harry on his Firebolt, and the Flash. Three laps. Who wins?"

Um, the Flash. Obviously.

Mom sighed. "I need to get him back on track. You think about it. I'll be back."

If it's only three laps, Harry would be second—

"Lexi," Mom added, "think about what you want Santa to bring. Got it?"

How does she always know?

What to ask Santa for felt like a big decision. I had never played with the usual stuff like games and dolls.

I tried to concentrate but was distracted by The Cat, who was halfway up our Christmas tree staring down at Luke.

Luke had completely lost interest in him again. I wondered if The Cat could write, would he ask Santa for a love potion that lasted longer than butter? Did Santa bring that kind of gift? Ones that couldn't be wrapped?

That was it! I could ask Santa to help with my gifts. He was numero uno in the gift-giving world. If he couldn't help, no one could.

That afternoon, Mom drove me to the outlet mall. She loaded me in my chair in the parking lot. I had barely used the chair since that day at the farm, probably because I had thrown such a god-awful fit in it. But I guess Mom wasn't up for Christmas week at the mall with a squirming kid in her arms. We rolled through the crush of shoppers, the letter crumpled in my fist.

Finally, I saw the tree towering over the crowd. A ginormous line snaked around the base. Mom rolled me to the back then held my head so I could see the decorations. Humongous presents rested on a blanket of felt snow. Two plastic elves stood on ladders, waving mechanically as "Santa Claus Is Comin' to Town" crackled over speakers.

The line inched forward. As my imagination heated up, my arms began to tingle.

Welcome to the Charlotte Motor Speedway and the first annual Speederrr Cuuulassic. In lane one, the big guy himself, Santaaaa Claus. In lane two, Mr. Magic, Harrrry Potter. And in lane three, the one, the only, the FuuuLASH!

I pump my arms. The crowd goes bananas.

The announcer holds the starting gun to the sky. "Runners and umm . . . fliers . . . Take your marks!"

BOOM!

Harry and Santa take off. I plop down on the starting line and retie my shoes. Twice. The crowd buzzes. I stretch and comb my hair.

Someone yells, "Whatcha waitin' for, Flash? Christmas?"

The crowd roars. I break into a jog, then I'm a streak of red.

I pass Harry and the old guy once, twice, three times then BAM! Cross the finish line.

The crowd chants, "Flash! Flash! Flash!"

"Lexi, look! There he is!"

What? Santa? Where?

I squealed so loud the entire line turned around, but when Mom turned my chair for me to see, my arms flopped. This Santa was a fake. *Obviously.* He had red painted cheeks and a glittery beard.

A man and woman were trying to bribe a wailing toddler onto his lap. Santa waited, slumped on his king-sized throne. And was that gum he was chewing?

Santa coughed and glanced at his watch. A lady dressed as an elf scurried from behind the counter. She jingled a stuffed reindeer in the boy's face, and he screamed even louder.

When the family moved to the checkout area, the elf-lady waved us in.

Santa looked me over. "So . . . what's her deal?"

"*Excuse* me?" Mom positioned herself between me and Santa.

Santa pointed a single, gloved finger at me. "What's up with her?"

For a hot second, I was back at the Renaissance Fair, flailing and sweaty, the little girl pointing at me and demanding, "What's wrong with her?"

I wanted to leave, needed to get out of there. But my letter! I had to get my letter to Santa. Even though this wasn't the real Santa, it was my only hope to get him my message.

Mom's fingers trembled as she rebuckled my seat harness. *Ggguuhhh.*

She looked at me. My eyes pleaded with hers.

"Are you sure? *Him?*"

Tongue out.

"Okay. But do you want to sit in his lap?"

Ggguuhhh.

She wheeled me closer. "Lexi has a letter she wrote *Santa*," she said, glaring.

Santa sat up straight, and I think swallowed his gum.

The elf-lady jingled the stuffed reindeer and said, "Let's get that picture! Are we buying the full package or—"

"We won't be buying pictures," Mom interrupted. "Lexi just wants to give *Santa* her letter."

She extended my arm.

Santa pried the letter from my hand.

"Read it," said Mom.

He cleared his throat. "'Dear Santa, I want you to bring me a gift. Love, Lexi.' Well, of course Santa will bring you a gift. How about a nice doll?"

Ggguuhhh!

Mom shook her head.

"Or something else." He looked at Mom and she nodded. "I'm sure Santa will think of something else. So, umm . . . Merry Christmas and be good!"

As Mom wheeled me toward the exit, I heard Santa say, "Doreen, hold the line. I need a smoke."

Mom mumbled, "I guess that's the Santa you get at the outlet mall."

CHAPTER 21

Age 5, The Year of the Buttered Cat

I wasn't sure how Santa would help with my gift situation, so I wasn't disappointed when the only gifts I found under the tree Christmas morning were *actual* gifts—a pair of Clone Wars Nerf blasters, the final *Harry Potter* book on CD, and an expansion pack of plastic letters with punctuation.

Kali said self-discovery is done privately, I reminded myself. If Santa was gonna help, it wouldn't be obvious. He would be subtle, maybe even a little sneaky. I had to pay attention.

The week between Christmas and New Year's turned cold and rainy. With Kali's help, I battled Tucker with my Nerf blasters. I listened to my new book and played around with the punctuation for my plastic letters. My favorites were the quotation marks. They were tiny but powerful. Two of them could corral an entire sentence or paragraph, like tiny sheepdogs on a cattle ranch.

One afternoon, when Hannah sat down to spell with me, I discovered they were also the most entertaining members of the punctuation family.

Hannah: "What do you want to do now?"

Me: **"What do you want to do now?"**

Hannah: "Let's play Hangman."

Me: **"Let's play Hangman."**

Hannah: "Are you copying me?"

Me: **"Are you copying me?"**

Hannah: "Stop it."

Me: **"Stop it."**

Hannah pushed away the cookie sheet. "I will spell with you under one condition."

I liked the pajamas-till-noon pace of the holidays, but by January, I was ready for school. On the first day of French, Mom decided I should finally try using my wheelchair in class.

My classmates admired the sparkly blue paint and took turns wheeling me around the room. Even Avery and Marc spun me in circles. When I got dizzy and let out one of my high-pitched *ggguuhhh*s, the boys stared in amazement.

"Whoa, Lexi! You sound *just* like Chewbacca!" Marc said.

Ms. Joann pulled out a bin of construction paper and markers and told us to make decorations for my wheels. Then she, Mom and Ms. Trejo went in the kitchen to drink tea. It was weird because all the kids were speaking English on *that* side of the red line.

At first, Anna tried to fix it by saying, "*Non, non, non! Parlez en français!*" but no one listened. She finally gave up and started talking in English too.

After a while, the grown-ups came back into the classroom, and Ms. Joann shuffled through papers on her desk.

Just before class started, Ms. Trejo put a hand on Mom's shoulder. "How about if the girls and I bring dinner over tonight?"

"No, no," Mom said, waving her hands. "Please don't go out of your way."

"It's not! I roasted a chicken, but Dean's been called out of town. Now it's just me and the girls. It'll help *me* to mess up *your* kitchen."

Mom laughed. "I guess I can't say no to that!"

We were gonna have *guests*? At our *house*? I wasn't sure how I felt about that. I mean I *liked* the Trejos and all, but at my *house*? It was sorta like the time I saw Ms. Joann in Target. Different worlds—each *thriving* on their own—should be kept separate. Otherwise, it's all awkward and stuff.

Ms. Joann told us all to take our seats. Avery pointed out I had already taken mine, and we all laughed. Ms. Joann said her prayers for us just like she always did, but today, she also said one for Mom. And, yeah, that was *super* weird because she wasn't even a student or anything.

We finally got down to French. Today we were studying *lettres muettes*, or silent letters. Ms. Joann explained that some letters are not pronounced at the end of French words; they are silent, or *muet*, and today we would be learning about five of these letters.

"*Répétez, s'il vous plaît: Muet S, muet D, muet T, muet X, muet P.*"

The class recited her list and, in my head, I did too.

Then, for emphasis, she had us repeat it in English. "Silent S, silent D, silent T, silent X, silent P."

I caught Mom's eye and shuffled in my wheelchair.

"What?" she whispered.

I shifted my eyes toward the bathroom.

"Do you have to go?"

Tongue out.

Mom wheeled me to the bathroom. She wrestled me through the door and onto the toilet seat. After several minutes she sighed. "Lexi, are you going or not?"

I had already gone and was waiting for her help with the, umm . . . *finale*. I uncurled a finger and pointed to the tissue roll.

"Oh, sorry," said Mom. She reached for the tissue. "I didn't hear anything."

The words sprang into my head and I guess found the trap door. Without thinking, I arched my back and hissed them out. "Silent pee!"

The shock of that joke coming from *my* mouth must have

been too much for Mom. She toppled backwards, and in a flash, we were on the floor, my legs tangled in hers. Mom was still clutching the end of the tissue. A long piece had unwound and was coiled around my arms.

For a hot second, we lay there completely silent like we had been tased or something. Then Mom started to giggle, which got me going, and all that laughing did nothing for getting us up off that floor.

Finally, there was a knock on the door.

"Is everything okay in there?" asked Ms. Joann.

"We're fine," Mom said, struggling to her feet. Then she whispered, "Lexi, you have the greatest sense of humor!"

I gasped. Did that just happen? After six long months, did my third gift appear to me on the *toilet*? Well played, humor. Well played. What else could rear up and knock me over—literally—as if to say, "Pay attention!"

I don't remember anything else about class that day. My head was filled with thoughts of gifts. *My* gifts. Finally.

Three down, two to go. And then my body will be here.

At home, Mom put me in my wheelchair so she could move me around easily while she cleaned. Tucker carried all the books from the kitchen table to the den. Mom and Hannah took down the good dishes—the *Thanksgiving* dishes—and washed them.

I watched without really paying attention.

I was happy to have finally discovered a gift, but where was the relief? I had expected it to wash over me like a good hard rain, flooding out all my doubts and fears. But to be totally honest, coming one step closer to my goal made my stomach a little queasy. I couldn't tell if it was because of excitement or worry.

Mom's cell buzzed from the kitchen table. She was smiling as she set out the plates, but when she glanced down her face went cold. She stared at the phone like it was a rattlesnake. Her hand inched toward it, then pulled back to her chest. All at once she snatched the phone from the table.

"Hello, Lou. Yes, yes . . . it *has* been a long time since we last talked."

CHAPTER 22
Age 13, 14 hours until surgery

"Hi, Haas family!" the receptionist at the Ronald McDonald House greets us. "How's your day been so far?"

"Long!" says Mom, "but I think those brownies might help."

We follow our noses to the kitchen, and Dad serves three brownies onto napkins.

There are two other families in the dining room.

Katy, pale and thin, picks at her brownie as her mom tells her to eat. Her sleek bald head is different from the one I'll be rocking tomorrow. I pump my arm, and she waves back, shyly.

A boy with a chocolate-covered face runs over to greet us.

"Hi, Eddie," Mom says. "How was dialysis today?"

"Good," says Eddie.

He plops onto the floor next to Gus and throws his arms around his neck. Gus licks the chocolate from Eddie's face and nuzzles his ear. I laugh.

Technically, as a service dog, Gus shouldn't be doing this, but in this house Mom and Dad don't enforce the rules.

I stare at the brownies while my parents chat with Eddie's mom.

Dad's phone pings in his pocket—a Facebook message ping.

I squirm—*please! It has to be*—but Dad doesn't make a move. I drink in deep gulps of air. Dad turns toward me, gives me his don't-even-think-about-it look, and returns to the conversation.

I hold in the belch as long as I can. When I'm about to explode, I let it out in a series of small burps that I hope Dad won't hear. Eddie does, though, so I have some fun making him laugh. Finally, Eddie and his mom head back upstairs.

Mom feeds me my brownie, but Dad waits an unnecessarily long time before fishing his phone from his pocket.

When he does, he makes a point of checking his email first. Finally, he looks up and says. "I suppose you want to hear your message."

I'm too tired to answer, so I stick out my tongue.

Dad touches the screen then reads, "Leslie from Long Island says, 'This surgery sounds painful. How will you handle that?'"

Mom and Dad exchange looks, and before they say a word,

I know, I *know* they aren't going to read me any more messages. *My* messages.

I screech, and my arm goes wild. Gus jumps up and tries to quiet me. He licks my face.

Mom pulls out my cookie sheet, and I don't even care that we're in public. I write: **I am 13.**

I can't manage more but it's okay. They know the rest. *I can fight my own battles.*

Upstairs, Mom positions my chair in front of the TV and flips through channels, but I'm not watching. I'm thinking about Long Island Leslie.

I want to tell her that brains don't have pain receptors, so you can poke around inside all you want without it hurting. But that would be a half truth. The other part, where they connect the leads in my brain to the battery in my stomach, hurts like a beast. First surgery, the pain took me by surprise. This time, I'm prepared.

Morphine works great if I don't wait too long to ask, but if the pain really cranks up, nothing helps. I need to break up the two-person fistfight before it turns into a citywide brawl. My family helped me work out a plan for how I can tell them when I need more pain meds. One hand squeeze means I need a pump of morphine, two squeezes means two pumps, and three means Bring. It. On.

I can't tell Long Island Leslie all that, and I even if I could, I wouldn't. I decide just to leave it right there.

Some cooking show I used to like last year is on TV. *Geez. Do these people know me at all?*

I focus instead on the banner strung over my window. Letters cut from construction paper are strung together like a Christmas garland. It says, *We Love You Lexi.*

Anna and Elle made it. They gave it to me at my hat party. I bet it took forever to cut out each one of those letters. I picture them fighting over what size and color they should be. That makes me laugh, then I sigh.

Why haven't you written me yet? You promised.

Gus pads over and drops a ball in my lap.

"I think he's trying to tell you something," Dad says. "Should we take him out to play for a few?"

I stick out my tongue. Right now, a distraction sounds great.

Deep breath in. My story. Breath out.

CHAPTER 23
Age 5, The Year of the Buttered Cat

Mom sunk into a chair at the kitchen table, her phone still to her ear.

I leaned hard toward her hoping to hear Lou's voice. I hoped it would be deep and confident. Like Superman. I pictured Lou standing on top of a building, his cape blowing behind him, and his cell tucked under his chin.

As it turned out, Mom was holding the phone so close I couldn't hear anything at all. At first, she didn't do any talking. She just sat there nodding.

Finally, she took in a deep breath. "Okay. I'll pass that on to Ken. But don't forget, Lou. The clock is ticking. We're nearly halfway to her deadline."

She shook her head and tossed her phone on the table. I stared in disbelief.

Her deadline?

My search didn't have a deadline. Did it? I thought back to the teenagers at Mitey Riders—still waiting for their bodies after all these years.

Did they miss the deadline for finding their gifts?

I tried to push that out of my mind. That's not what Mom and Lou were talking about. There was no deadline, no ticking clock for finding my gifts and getting my body. *Obviously.*

I repeated my gift count. *Three down, two to go. And then my body will be here.* But this time, something else jumped in behind that, and no matter how hard I tried, I couldn't make it go away: *Tick. Tick. Tick.*

When the Trejos arrived at six, I was still in my chair. Anna and Elle stole me from the kitchen and rolled me into my room. I watched them stage lightsaber duels with my Star Wars action figures and flip through my Marvel comics. Only my family had ever been in my room before. Touched my stuff.

I knew this was gonna be weird.

"You like superheroes?" Elle finally asked, admiring the Spider-Man, Thor, and Hulk posters hanging over my bed.

Tongue out.

"Me too."

"Not me," said Anna. "I like wizards."

"Yeah, but Mom won't let us read *Harry Potter* books yet," Elle said with a sigh.

I uncurled my finger and pointed to the stack of *Harry Potter* books by my bed.

"Wow, Lexi! You're so lucky!"

I smiled.

They dumped all seven books on my bed then stood back like they were admiring their Halloween candy loot.

Anna picked up *The Chamber of Secrets* and ran her hand over the cover. Then she saw *The Prisoner of Azkaban* and grabbed that instead.

Elle had picked up *The Sorcerer's Stone* and was curled on my bed, happily devouring the first pages.

Anna gasped. "Mom said you can't read it till you're ten! I'm telling!"

Elle sighed. She closed the book and held it tight to her chest. "Which is your favorite, Lexi?"

I pointed to *The Prisoner of Azkaban*, which Anna was cradling like a new baby.

"What's that he's riding?" Anna asked, pointing to the cover.

I pointed to a poster by my desk.

"Magical Beasts," Elle read. She scanned it and said, "Oh! It's a hippo . . . a hippogrr—eyeff?"

Ggguuhhh.

"Hippo*grief*?" guessed Anna.

*Hippo*GRIFF! *It's a hippo*GRIFF! If only I could tell them!

"Girls, dinner!" Mom called, and they rolled me into the kitchen.

As we ate, Mom told the whole Silent Pee story, which

was sort of embarrassing, but I was proud that everyone knew about my third gift.

"Lexi finds humor in everything," Kali said.

"She's definitely her father's child," agreed Mom. "Tucker, eat your spinach."

Dad picked up my hand and high-fived me.

"Maybe you'll have a career in comedy," Ms. Trejo pointed out.

"Yeah!" Kasey agreed. "You could write for *SNL*."

"What's *SNL*?" asked Anna.

"A show you aren't allowed to watch yet," Ms. Trejo said.

Elle was right. I *was* lucky. I had free access to both *Harry Potter* and *SNL*.

"But who would push her chair at work?" Hannah asked.

"She'll have an assistant for stuff like that," Kali said. "Or maybe she'll have a motorized chair she can drive herself. Please pass the chicken."

Motorized chair? Assistant? When did everyone decide I'll need THOSE? Please! My gifts! Talk about my gifts!

Didn't they understand? My gifts were a sign that my body was on its way. Two more and it would be here! But Ms. Trejo and my parents were talking about wheelchairs and colleges. No one noticed my flailing arm.

I tried to escape into a fantasy—somewhere, *anywhere*—

but for the first time ever, it didn't work. No superheroes came to my rescue.

I felt like I had stepped into quicksand. The more I flailed, the deeper I sunk.

"And how about those arms? Who's gonna hold those down for her?" Tucker said. "Throw me the ketchup."

"*Pass* Tucker the ketchup," Mom said.

I flailed harder.

Stop it! This is stupid! YOU'RE stupid. You don't get it. Maybe it IS taking longer than I thought, but I'm figuring out my gifts. Two more and my body will be here. Two. More.

The *tick, tick, tick* grew louder. My arm hit Kasey's fork, sending it sailing across the kitchen. The table went quiet, and everyone stared at me. I glared back.

"What's wrong?" Kali asked.

Anna and Elle looked into their napkins, and for a hot second, I was ashamed.

Tucker shrugged and said, "Maybe she wants to work someplace else. Maybe she wants to work at Cartoon Network."

I arched hard and screeched.

"Okay, okay, no Cartoon Network," said Kasey. "I'm sure your wheelchair can go any place you want. There's rules about that, you know."

No! Mom! Dad! Tell them about me catching up! Tell them my body is coming in, and I'll catch up.

Mom rubbed her temples, and I knew my message was getting through.

Mom! Please. Tell them.

Right at that moment, The Cat bounded into the kitchen with Luke hot on his heels. They looped the kitchen island. Luke barked and growled. The Cat hissed and yowled. Finally, The Cat took a ginormous leap and landed on the table, smack in the middle of the mashed potatoes. Luke jumped up, his front paws on the table, and barked.

Anna and Elle leaned back and stared, wide-eyed, until Ms. Trejo said, "And this is why we only have a bunny."

Everyone laughed except for Dad. He threw his napkin on the table and plucked The Cat from the potato dish. "I am fed up with you two arguing like an old married couple."

He tossed The Cat onto the back porch. Luke ran out behind him.

"You two can stay out here until you learn to get along!"

"I think they already have," Kali said, under her breath.

Through the window I could see The Cat curled on his back and Luke hunched over him, licking potatoes from his paws.

"Please pass the potatoes," said Tucker.

"Gross," said Hannah.

After that, dinner continued as if nothing unusual had happened. Luke smooshed his nose against the window and looked so sad, we all felt sorry for him—except Dad. He would look out at him every so often and shake his finger.

As our guests got ready to leave, Ms. Trejo said, "Maybe the girls could come over to work on homework once a week. The National French Exam is coming up soon. They could study for it together."

"That sounds like . . . like fun," said Mom, but I could tell she and I were on the same page.

Once was fine—I mean we survived it and all—but *every* week? Besides, I had work to do. I still had two more gifts that had to be found. Fast!

"Well, Mondays the girls have Bible study and Tuesday is French," said Ms. Trejo. "How's Wednesday afternoon? We could start tomorrow."

"Tomorrow?" said Mom. "I think we have something then."

"Whadaya mean?" said Tucker. "We never have anything on Wednesdays. It's the number one boringest day of the week."

"Then tomorrow works?" Ms. Trejo asked.

Mom smiled. "Tomorrow is fine."

"Oh, I forgot something," Anna said. She ran over to me and whispered, "This is for you, Lexi."

She pressed a small rock into my hand and curled my

fingers around it. I couldn't see it, but as I studied it with my fingers, I decided it felt *gray*—like an ordinary old rock. It had rough edges that smooshed into my palm.

Mom stood at the door and waved. Luke sneaked in with his tail between his legs. The Cat pranced in behind him like he owned the place.

That night as Dad put me to bed, he uncurled my fingers. The rock had left little patterns in my palm.

"What's this?" he asked.

He held it up. I had been right. It was an ordinary piece of gravel—gray with little white flecks.

I laughed. Dad scratched his head. It was *my* secret.

As I drifted off to sleep, I imagined the feeling of the rock pressed into my palm. I had squeezed it so hard, every bump, every corner was burned into my memory. Why did she give me that? Was I supposed to do something with it? My stomach churned. I had no idea where Dad had put it! I took a deep breath. It couldn't have gone far. If I was supposed to do something with it, someone in my family could find it for me.

My family.

I was still mad at them for planning my grown-up life without my body, but right then, right at that moment, what *they* thought didn't count for anything. Besides, I'd show them. My body was coming. Now that I knew three gifts, it was closer than ever.

Three down, two to go. And then my body will be here. Tick. Tick. Tick.

CHAPTER 24
Age 5, The Year of the Buttered Cat

The afternoon after their first visit, Anna and Elle came back, this time lugging backpacks. Mom set us up at the computer to do some online test prep for the exam. After that, we slogged through vocab and conjugations. By the fourth worksheet, I was *over* French. That ticking clock that was not supposed to be there still was, and I had a hard time concentrating on anything else. Finally, I pretended to fall asleep.

The girls rolled me to Mom's office. I nailed my part, eyes shut tight and head drooped to one side.

"Mrs. Haas, can we stop now?" Anna asked. "Lexi's tired."

I opened one eye, just a tiny bit. Mom eyed me with her head tilted.

After a long moment she smiled and said, "Why don't you girls hang out in Lexi's room."

"Way to go, Lexi," Elle whispered as she rolled me to my room.

They shut my door behind us. Anna jumped up on my bed. Elle clicked my lightsaber on and off like ten times in a row so that it made that whoosh power-on noise over and over. That weird feeling of having something alien in my space came back and sat on my chest like an Ewok.

Finally, Anna said, "Cut it out, Elle."

Elle stabbed her with the lightsaber then with an, "Ohhh," dropped it and grabbed *Harry Potter and The Sorcerer's Stone* from my nightstand. She ran her hand over the cover then opened it, just a tiny bit, like she was afraid an owl or a dragon might fly out.

She glanced up. In one motion, she flipped open the cover and sputtered the words out, like she had dived headfirst into icy water. "Mr. and Mrs. Dursley of number four, Privet Drive, were proud to say that they were perfectly normal, thank you very much."

"Elle, no! We aren't supposed to read them yet."

Elle stopped talking, but from the way her eyes were moving back and forth, I knew she was finding out about the Dursleys' secret.

Anna reached over and snapped the book shut.

"Ow, that was my hand, Anna!"

"We'll get in trouble."

"Not if Mom doesn't find out."

I knew exactly how to fix this, but they were off in their own world. I drank in deep breaths and let out a long burp. They turned to face me.

"What was that?" Anna said, giggling.

I uncurled a finger and pointed to a pile of *Harry Potter* CDs on my desk.

Elle grabbed them. "She said we couldn't *read* them, but she didn't say we couldn't *listen* to them. Lexi, you're a genius!"

Obviously.

She closed my door and popped the first CD into the player.

"Elle, if Mom finds out we're gonna be . . . in . . . big . . ."

Anna slumped onto my bed like she was under the Imperius Curse or something. No one said a word until the CD ended.

Elle was putting in the second one when my door flew open.

"What're you doing in here?" Tucker demanded.

"Nothing," Elle said.

"Mom wants to know if you want a snack."

"No!" Anna and Elle barked.

Ggguuhhh.

"Oookay. Geez!" He backed away.

Elle locked the door behind him and popped in the second CD.

The doorknob jiggled.

"Lexi, I know you're up to something."

"We're just listening to books," Elle said.

"It's not fair. I don't get to lock *my* door."

The doorknob jiggled harder, then suddenly stopped.

Elle reached for the CD player.

Ggguuhhh. I pointed toward the door. There was no way he would give up that easy.

"He's gone," Anna said.

Ggguuhhh.

The knob jiggled again. A note slid under the door.

"Surrender now or suffer the consequences," Elle read.

Ggguuhhh.

"I heard that," Tucker said.

Footsteps faded down the hall. Anna and Elle high-fived each other.

Ggguuhhh.

"He's coming back, isn't he?" Elle said.

Tongue out.

I pointed toward my toy box. Anna and Elle picked through it, holding up my stuffed owl. *Ggguuhhh.* A Spider-Man mask. *Ggguuhhh.*

There was a new sound at the doorknob, this one fainter—metal against metal. A coat hanger? Was he picking my lock?

Oh, it is on.

I pointed frantically to my desk. Anna picked up the CD player.

Ggguuhhh.

She pointed to my corkboard and my desk lamp then threw up her hands. "I don't know what you want, Lexi."

Ugghhh. This would be so much easier if I could just—

The door lock popped open. Elle quickly pushed it back in.

I flailed and pointed again.

"This?" Anna asked. She held up my cookie sheet.

Tongue out.

No one outside of my family had ever helped me spell before, but desperate times called for desperate measures.

Anna held the board in my lap. Elle held my wrist.

I put my finger on the **N**. It wouldn't budge. Elle had my wrist clamped too tight. I pointed again. Anna grabbed it and stuck it at the bottom.

I tried for the second letter, but my hand couldn't reach.

Don't hold so tight, I tried to tell Elle telepathically, but she just squeezed harder.

"A?" Anna guessed.

Ggguuhhh

"E?" asked Elle.

Tongue out.

The door lock popped again. This time Anna lunged and pushed it back in.

"It's only a matter of time," Tucker said, in his creepy villain voice.

I moved my hand, this time all the way to the right, and Elle's grip loosened. In one pass, I pointed to the **R**, then the **F**.

Anna added them to the first two.

"Nerf," Elle read.

I pointed to my toy box.

Anna dove for the box and threw toys across the room. Finally, she held up two Clone Wars Nerf blasters. I squealed. She tossed one to Elle.

The lock popped open, and Tucker flung open the door.

"Fire!" Elle cried.

Two Nerf darts hit him in the stomach. They reloaded and fired again. Tucker wrestled a blaster from Anna.

"Tucker, are you bothering the girls?" Mom called.

He shot a dart at Elle. "Mom! Why do you always take her side? She's not an angel, you know. She can be bad too."

He reloaded.

"Did you finish those math problems?" Mom asked.

Tucker groaned. He tossed the blaster on my bed.

Elle shot another dart and hit him in the butt.

"Not an angel," he called back.

Elle picked up my hand and high-fived me. "That was amazing."

"Lexi," Anna said, "you're a good friend."

She leaned over and hugged me. I smiled.

That night when Dad put me to bed, I replayed our epic battle over and over in my head. Even more, I replayed Anna's words. *Lexi, you're a good friend.*

I squeezed my imaginary rock. I had been wrong. This was not an ordinary rock. This was what a friend felt like.

I let the newness of that settle in. What kind of stuff do you even do with friends? Epic battles and shared secrets, *obviously*. But it seemed like there was more to it than that. Friends were always there for each other. You help them with *Harry Potter*, and they help you with . . . *What?* A little internet search? One that might dig up some information about Lou Lattimore?

CHAPTER 25
Age 13, 13 hours until surgery

In the field beside the Ronald McDonald House, Dad chucks a tennis ball as hard as he can. Gus tears out after it. The ball bounces softly in the grass, and Gus lunges hard to catch it in his mouth. He turns around smiling and shows us he stopped it. Then he drops it and lies down on top.

I think he's having one of his superhero fantasies again. *Gus, the Amazing Labrador Receiver.* There's no retriever in him. It's all about the chase. Frisbees, balls, arms.

Dad whistles twice. Gus picks up the ball and trots back.

Mom and I are watching from beneath a tree. I can see storm clouds in the distance, but our patch of earth is sunny and warm.

A few days ago, when we flew in from Charlotte, I scored a seat by the window. Propped up with pillows, I watched the earth below us disappear into the clouds. Occasionally, we would fly low enough to see the ground again. When we did, I focused on the shadows the clouds cast on the ground below.

Right there, straight below me, people were waking up to a cloudy day and making plans for the library or the movies. I shifted my eyes. And right over there, they were waking up to sun and planning for the pool. *How cool is Earth?*

Toward the end of our flight, the landscape became endless green folds—the Ozark Mountains according to Dad, although they looked much less like mountains than the ones in North Carolina.

The man seated behind me must have overheard because he said, "Ozarks indeed and just below us is the Sunklands."

Dad swiveled around. The man reached his hand between our seats and shook Dad's hand.

"Name's Bob. I work for the parks department right here in the Show-Me State. Those Sunklands are somethin' else. Named for all the sinkholes down there. One's over a mile long."

The Show-Me State might as well have been called the Tell-Me State, because for the rest of the flight Bob pumped us with all the information we would ever need about sinkholes. For example, did you know that Missouri is one of the most sinkhole-prone states in the country? And, fun fact, sinkholes don't happen just anywhere. They happen in places where the rock below the surface has eroded away, leaving a cavity that will eventually collapse in on itself.

When we finally landed, Bob gave Dad a business card and told him if we ever wanted to tour an honest-to-goodness Missouri sinkhole, give him a call.

"And that means you too, little lady," he said, tipping his hat.

I smiled at him and thought, *I have a close-up view of my own personal sinkhole, thank you very much.*

Bob held back the line of passengers so Mom and Dad could shimmy out into the narrow aisle with me. Dad carried me out to the jetway, then he and Mom took turns holding me upright as we waited for the ground crew to bring up my wheelchair.

The jetway was hot and steamy, and my legs felt shaky. With my feet planted firmly in Kansas City, I was sure I could feel the rock eroding beneath me. This was Ground Zero for my surgery, and it was all getting too real too fast. My own honest-to-goodness Missouri sinkhole bubbled and churned beneath me, and for a hot second I thought my fears would swallow me whole right then and there.

Two stocky men in yellow vests heaved my wheelchair onto the jetway. Mom and Dad whisked me up off my feet and into my chair. Dad popped a wheelie and ran with me up the jetway into the air-conditioning.

I hoped I would see Bob again. I wanted to fly past him and shout, "Fun fact: wheelies can tame Missouri sinkholes!"

But Bob, Fellow Sinkhole Warrior, was gone.

A breeze—much softer than the one at the memorial—rustles the leaves on my tree and tickles my face, bringing me back to the field at the Ronald McDonald House. Right now, I'm so content I want to grow roots and stay here in this spot forever.

But then the rustle becomes a whisper, *Hurry, hurry.*

Deep breath in. My story. Breath out.

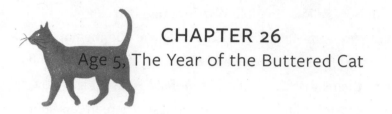

CHAPTER 26
Age 5, The Year of the Buttered Cat

The next Wednesday, after Anna, Elle, and I finished our on-line test prep, I pointed to my spelling board.

Elle picked it up. "Do you have something to say? Want me to get your mom?"

Ggguuhhh. I arched and grimaced.

"Okay, okay! No mom. We can do this."

Anna held the cookie sheet on my lap, and Elle held my wrist. It took a few minutes to find a rhythm, but when I was done, I took a deep breath. My arm went limp.

"Look up Lou Lattimore," Anna read, a little too loud.

Ggguuhhh. I reached forward again and pulled down **Shh**.

"Who's Lou Lattimore?" whispered Elle.

Ggguuhhh.

"You don't know?"

Tongue out. I pointed toward the computer.

Elle shrugged, then sat in front of the keyboard. After a minute she announced, "The only Lou Lattimore that comes up is a dress shop in Texas."

"Let me try," Anna said, pushing Elle from the computer. "Maybe Lou is short for something else."

"Good idea. Try Louis Lattimore," Elle suggested.

Nothing came up for Louis, Lucas, or Lucius Lattimore. Apparently, there was an American inventor named Lewis Lattimore, but he died in 1928.

"Maybe it's a pseudonym," Elle said.

"A pseudowhat?" asked Anna.

"You know, an alias or false name. Like J. K. Rowling. That isn't her real name. It's a pseudonym."

There was a knock at the front door.

"Anna. Elle," Mom called. "Your mom's here."

Elle closed the web page. "Anyway, think about it. Then maybe we can look again. But next week, you owe me a double dose of *The Sorcerer's Stone*."

After they left, I considered the pseudonym angle. As crazy as it sounded, Lou Lattimore might actually be a real-life superhero. I mean, he had an alias that was *nowhere* to be found online. He was determined to help me get back my missing things. Why wasn't Mom on board with it? She knew about the deadline and that it was getting closer.

With no luck tracking down Lou Lattimore, that *tick, tick, tick* grew louder and more persistent.

In early February, my class took the National French Exam. Mom held my wrists while I pointed to answers on my test booklet. The test was pretty easy, I thought, and Anna and Elle agreed. Now I could finally focus on my missing things.

One morning in late February, I was awakened by a hand placed softly on my cheek.

"Lexi," Mom whispered.

I opened one eye and saw pink sunrise filtered through frost-covered windows. I shivered and shut my eye.

Mom jostled me.

Ggguuhhh.

"C'mon, Lex. We have an appointment at the Center this morning, so we need to get moving."

I arched my back and grimaced.

Mom laughed. "I think you're being a little dramatic. The Center isn't so bad, and Celeste really likes you."

I groaned. I hadn't been to the Assistive Technology Center since last summer. Hadn't everyone finally given up on that?

"I know it's frustrating, but Celeste says now that you have your chair it might be easier to use a communication device. She has a new one for us try today."

Of course. A new one. Trouble was, there was *always* a new one. A new device that would talk for me until my voice came in. But they never worked the way they said they would. Celeste, the speech pathologist at the Center, had let me borrow at least five different devices, but none of them had worked for me. I just didn't have enough control of my muscles yet.

I already had that nonstop ticking clock. I didn't need any more reminders about my missing body. Just thinking about the Center made me so stiff Mom couldn't get my coat on me.

"Take a deep breath," Mom instructed.

I breathed in, and Mom quickly pulled my arm through the sleeve.

On the way, Mom said, "Wouldn't it be great if you could use a device to talk to the girls? You could bring it in your room for . . . for whatever it is you three do in there."

I grinned. The fact that she didn't know made me feel a tiny bit better. I squeezed my imaginary rock until the edges dug into my skin.

"You know, we can probably mount a device on your wheelchair, and you'll be able to use it all the time!"

All the time? No! I wanted my voice! My *real* voice.

I stared at my sticker collection and the spitball still hanging from Hulk's nose. *Stupid Tucker. He ruined the Hulk. MY Hulk.*

I could feel the heat growing under my coat. I did *not* want to be going to the Center. I did not want a device mounted on my wheelchair. I did *not* want a spitball stuck on Hulk's nose.

My arms began to tingle.

Rrrripp . . . Wow! I didn't know a coat could actually explode! Crunch! And there goes my car seat, flattened like an empty juice box. Dad's gonna have a cow when he finds out I've smooshed another one. Grrreen hands! Grrr . . . Hulk. No. Go. Center. Hulk save world.

At the Center, Mom rolled me up to the door. A sign read, *The North Carolina Assistive Technology Program. Please ring bell for assistance.*

My arm flew out and Mom held my wrist while I pushed the button.

"Hey there, Buttercup! I love your new chair!" said Celeste.

She pulled off my hat and pretended to crack an egg on my head. I didn't want to laugh, but I couldn't help myself.

"I have something new for you to try today."

She rolled me into a back room filled with all sorts of equipment—telephones for people who couldn't hear, books for people who couldn't see, and even toys for kids who were still waiting for their bodies.

We stopped at what looked like a big tablet computer mounted on an aluminum stand. Celeste pushed a button, and a familiar picture grid flashed on the screen.

This grid had been on every device I borrowed from the Center. The pictures represented real words and were meant to be a time-saver, but getting to the right picture was a nightmare for someone with no muscle control.

I arched and grimaced.

"Now hold up! This is completely different from devices you've used before. It has little cameras inside that follow your eyes. All you need to do is look at the button you want, and the device will pick it for you. It's also touch-sensitive, which makes it easy for people to help."

She touched several buttons on the control page, and a keyboard appeared on the screen. "I thought you might like to spell instead of using the pictures for a change. So it's more like your cookie sheet."

I stopped grimacing. *Spell?*

Celeste touched the *L*, *E*, *X* and *I* buttons. The computer announced each letter. She touched the top bar, and a voice said "Lexi."

I smiled.

"Why don't you give it a try?"

She stepped back so I could see the screen, but my head twisted hard to the side.

Mom shook out my arms then slowly coaxed my head back to the middle and held it there.

A cursor flashed on the screen. As my eyes moved, the cursor moved too. It looked like a ghost was operating the computer.

"You need to look directly at the letter you want and hold your eyes there for two seconds before the computer will pick it," Celeste said.

My eyes settled on the B. The device announced "B," and the letter appeared at the top. I was trying for the L, but it didn't matter. I had made it work. With my eyes!

I accidentally hit three more letters—R, A, and Z—before my eyes finally settled on the L. I looked at the top, and the computer said "Brazl," which made us all laugh.

"This is pretty cool," said Mom, "but it's no more independent than spelling in my lap."

"She can't sit in your lap and spell forever, Susan," Celeste said.

Forever? Let me tell you about forever, lady. When I know my gifts and my body comes in, I'll leave this place and all these stupid devices FOREVER.

I tried telepathic communication. *Tell her, Mom. Tell her that's what forever means.*

But Mom was rummaging in her bag.

"I'll tell you what," Celeste said. "She can borrow this. Give her time to practice, and let's see where she goes with it. It's cutting-edge technology that's helping all sorts of people get back some of what they've lost."

"Not lost," said Mom, "Stolen. But I've been thinking a lot about how to get some of it back." She held out a handful of dog-eared papers. "There's this devious procedure I've been researching, and I want to see what you think about it. It would be pretty radical, and maybe I'd regret it, but if by the end of the summer she doesn't show signs of catching up, I'd like to consider it."

Wait—what? Stolen? Devious procedure?

Had I really heard all that?

My mom was working on a plan to get something back from the thief—something that was keeping me from catching up. The theft and my missing body *were* related! And there was an *actual* deadline—*before the end of summer*.

Celeste made a copy of the papers. I watched Mom put the originals back in my bag. I needed to know her devious plan. I had to see those papers.

That afternoon, when Mom closed herself in her office, I pointed to my cookie sheet until Hannah finally agreed to spell with me.

As soon as we did, I wrote, **Mom has a devious plan.**

Hannah laughed. "Let me guess. You overheard this."

It's in my bag.

"The plan?"

Tongue out.

Hannah shook her head. She emptied the contents of my wheelchair bag onto the table—crackers, hand sanitizer, my sunglasses, and some dog-eared papers. I arched and pointed.

She unfolded the papers and read, "*Bilateral, pallidal, deep-brain stimulation in primary generalized dystonia: a prospective three-year follow-up study.* Yep, that sounds terrifying, Lexi. Absolutely devious."

She held the paper so I could see it.

"In case you haven't noticed, our mother is a *medical* writer. This is her *job*. I've told you before. You mishear stuff. All. The. Time."

I stared at the papers. I read the first few words of the title before my eyes darted in different directions. Hannah was right. This paper looked complicated and boring, but not devious.

Still, in the pit of my stomach, something didn't seem right. No way did I mishear *all* of what she said. She had definitely said that if I didn't catch up by the end of summer she would do something radical that she might regret.

I had to be alert for more clues.

But above all, I had to find my gifts. Before the end of summer. Before it was too late for my body to come in. Before Mom did something she might regret.

CHAPTER 27
Age 5, The Year of the Buttered Cat

I had a tradition of naming the communication devices Celeste sent home with me. It always took a few days to get to know a new device, and this one was no different. By the end of the first week, I had named this one Haha—good for some laughs, but that was about it. Each afternoon Mom wheeled me up to the kitchen table to practice. If I could hold my head and eyes just right, I could choose the letter I wanted, but the only button I could hit almost every time was the big one at the top.

On Wednesday, Anna and Elle came over. We had a lot less French homework now that the exam was done, so Mom suggested I introduce them to Haha.

She rolled me up to the table and held my head steady until the cursor appeared. I tried to type *hello*, but hit all the wrong buttons.

When I hit the top button, Haha said, "Jekklip."

Anna giggled. Elle elbowed her in the ribs, but I laughed too.

"Lemme try," Elle said.

She touched several letters. I activated the top button.

"Jekklip brklfsh."

"That's cool," Elle said. "It's like a game of Add On."

"My turn!" said Anna. She added her letters.

"Jekklip brklfsh pooklngr."

Anna and Elle kept adding mashed-up, made-up words to the top screen. Those crazy words sounded so *familiar* . . . like the made-up words Mr. Bean had chanted in that diner six months ago.

Six months ago. Six months to go. Tick. Tick. Tick.

The new deadline went off in my head so often, I had gotten used to it. Six months, after all, was way, way in the future. And there was Lou Lattimore. He was out there right now, flying over the city, looking for my missing things.

I pointed to my room. The girls wheeled me off to escape with Harry, Ron, and Hermione.

By Friday, I was totally over Haha. The day before, I had managed to spell *go* and *no*, but now I couldn't even turn my head for it to read my eyes. Kali was working on a homework assignment at the table. After I grunted and groaned for several minutes, she looked up.

"Lexi, would you like some help?"

Tongue out.

She reached over and tried to turn my head, but it was

stuck. She pressed one hand against my cheek and whispered in my ear, "Guess what happened at school today?"

My eyes met hers.

She smiled. "Someone pulled an alarm so the entire school had to stand outside in the freezing cold while the fire department checked it out. We didn't even get to put on our coats!"

I gasped. Kali gently moved my head toward the middle.

"The principal walked up and down the sidewalk and asked if anyone knew who had done it. No one said anything, but I think I know who it was."

I could feel my neck muscles relax and my head straighten.

"There's this kid in my chemistry class who's always causing trouble. I saw him outside and guess what? He was wearing his coat. I bet he did it!"

My head was now perfectly straight. The cursor popped up on the screen.

I wanted to tell Kali she should ask the kid if he had pulled the alarm. The cursor settled on the A long enough for Haha to say, "A." I moved my eyes over just a bit, and Haha announced, "S."

Two in a row! Now all I had to do was slide my eyes to the right six spaces, and I'd run smack into K. Five spaces. Four. Three. Two. My eyes suddenly darted back to the left and hit S again.

No! Not S!

My eyes bounced around the screen then hit the top button.

"Ass," Haha said.

Kali snorted. "Well, he's a bit of a jerk to make the whole school stand outside but, *wow*, Lexi! That's harsh!"

Kasey appeared in the kitchen and picked through a bowl of fruit on the counter.

I activated the top button again. "Ass."

Kasey's eyes widened as she bit into an apple.

I laughed and hit the button three times in a row.

"Ass-Ass-Ass."

I heard Mom's footsteps closing in from down the hall.

"Uh-oh! Now you've done it," Kali said.

"What did you say?" asked Mom.

I looked at the device.

"Ass."

Mom erased the screen. She glared at Kali.

"Hey, it's not my fault. You said you wanted her to talk. Well, now she's talking!"

"Yeah," Kasey said. "You can't exactly wash her eyes out with soap, can you?"

Mom shook a finger at me. "No more cursing!"

But I could tell there was a little smile behind her and-I-mean-it glare.

"I have an idea," Kasey said when Mom left. She touched letters on the screen. "Now say that."

I looked at the top button. Haha said, "Communication devices are what's wrong with America today."

We all laughed. Kasey turned up the volume. I hit it twice more.

Mom reappeared in the kitchen doorway, shaking her head but smiling.

"Get used to it, Mom," Kasey said. "She's here and she can't be censored."

That night I dreamed about computers. First, I was in Celeste's office. She was loading computers onto my lap and saying, "Maybe this one will work for you. Or this one!"

Then, out of the blue, hands reached toward me, and a voice hissed like water on a hot griddle, "Stolen, stolen, stolen."

The scene changed. I was sitting in Mom's lap in that island of soft, blue light from her computer. Everything else was pitch dark and completely quiet except for the *clickety-clack* of the keyboard. I don't know exactly how old I was, but I was tall enough to see the screen. We were at our house in Chapel Hill, so I guessed I was about one.

For a few minutes, this dream was nothing more than the familiar *clickety-clack, clickety-clack, stare, rock, rock.*

Clickety-clack, clickety-clack, stare, rock, rock. But then, Mom abruptly stopped typing, stopped rocking, and leaned in toward the computer.

One-year-old me looked up at the screen. Near the bottom was a picture of a man with a graying beard, bright, happy eyes, and a slightly crooked tie.

Was this the thief? I wanted a good, long look at that man, but it was too late. Baby me was now reaching for Luke, who was licking my toes.

I giggled and squirmed. Mom's grip tightened on my waist. She stood up fast, flung open the front door, and sat down hard with me on the porch steps.

The night air was cool and quiet. Luke nuzzled the grass in front of us. Mom breathed deeply and rocked me back and forth, but it wasn't the gentle rocking I knew so well. This rocking was hard and fast.

As she exhaled, she began to mumble softly—so softly I couldn't make out what she was saying. Bit by bit her voice grew until I realized she wasn't talking; she was praying.

"Oh, God! Please no! Please no! Don't let her . . . Oh, God."

Warm tears spilled onto my neck and trickled down my back.

All at once Mom stood up, leaned over the porch railing, and threw up.

It must have been the thumping in my chest that woke me. My heart pounded, like someone locked in a cellar, desperate to get out.

I knew one thing for certain: This wasn't a dream. It was a memory. A real one.

CHAPTER 28
Age 13, 12¾ hours until surgery

Dad's whistles have faded into the background and under this tree, I am very nearly asleep. It's in these moments of fragmented consciousness that I let my imagination off leash.

When I was younger and I dreamed of the things I would do when my body came in, they were always action packed. I cartwheeled down a beach. Outsprinted my friends in tag. Raced Tucker on a bike.

I used to think those early dreams were about chasing fun, but now I know better. They were about chasing identity. About defining myself. *I am a runner. I can jump.* After all, those things would help me fit neatly into the human prototype, right?

We call people who run crazy fast and jump extra high *superhuman*. Where does that leave me?

I'm not sure how or when I slogged through all that. It started with the gift prophecy, but as for *identity*? Yeah, work in progress.

I do know one thing: as I've gotten older, those action sequences have become less important. Now when I unleash my imagination, my dreams are nearly always about my voice.

Do you know what it's like when you hear your voice on a recording? How you shudder and think, *Do I really sound like that?*

I don't. I've never heard my voice. Sure, I've heard the quick bursts of words I can huff out since my last surgery, but those don't really have a voice. Those words are strained and gasping, like I'm coming up for air in a swimming pool.

I do have a voice inside my head, just like everyone else does, I guess. And I *think* that voice is what I would sound like, but I'm not sure.

My wildest, craziest dream is to hear my own voice played back to me on a recording. Would I have a Southern drawl? North Carolina twang? Would I sound smooth and sweet? Loud and shrill?

In this dream, I laugh or maybe cringe and say, "Is that really me?"

I listen to my recorded voice with my eyes closed, like I do when Mom plays a podcast on her phone. I concentrate on the rhythm, the tone, the pitch. And the words!

Words I have heard in my head forever, become real when they leave my lips.

When I've had my fill of talking, I test out my singing voice—jazz, rock, and maybe opera in falsetto.

After that, I try on my shouting voice, an earsplitting shriek so loud I have a sore throat when I'm done (is that really a thing?).

Then, I drop my voice so low you have to lean in, and I whisper a secret.

Out of nowhere, a panting, drooling furball punches through my nap like a linebacker through a paper banner. Gus is halfway on my lap, a slimy ball in his smiling mouth. I survey him with one eye.

"If it isn't Sleeping Beauty," Dad says. "Someone wants you to play too."

"There's a little playground at the hospital," Mom says. "Unless you're too old for that."

I stick out my tongue and smile. Right now, pretending I'm a little kid again sounds amazing.

Deep breath in. My story. Breath out.

CHAPTER 29
Age 5, The Year of the Buttered Cat

I don't know what Mom found on her computer that night, but I was sure of one thing. It was about me. She said, "Don't let *her.*" And yeah, there are a bunch of people in our house who could be *her*, but I knew by the way she hugged me—pressed to her chest, like she was scared if she let go she would lose me.

If that man in the computer was the thief, and the thief had the answer to my missing body . . . I had to know what this memory was about. But no matter how much I searched my brain, no more came.

Finally, I shifted my focus to the information pipeline on the other side of my bedroom wall. Maybe I would at least get an update on how Lou's search was going.

For several nights all I overheard was ordinary conversation. Sometimes Dad would sing his responses to Mom's comments, and I would bite my lower lip to keep from laughing out loud.

Mom: "Don't forget you have a dentist appointment to-morrow."

Dad (strumming "Hey Jude"):

"Hey Sue,

I won't forget

That tomorrow,

They'll clean my chomper-er-ers . . ."

But then one evening, as Gershwin's "Summertime" seeped through the walls and settled around me like a thick August night, Mom cut in, midtune.

"I have a confession."

Dad's guitar strummed out *dum, dum, duuummm* like he was announcing a thickening plot on a TV soap opera.

"No, seriously," Mom said, laughing. "This has been both-ering me, and I need to confess."

Confess?

The strumming stopped, and I imagined Dad leaning in on his guitar, just as I leaned toward my wall.

Mom drew a deep breath. "I buttered The Cat."

"What?"

"When The Cat finally came back last fall, I brought him into the garage and buttered him. Top to bottom."

"Why on earth—"

"Because I needed to fix something, even if that something

was as silly as the relationship between a dog and his cat." She paused, and I could hear muffled sobs. "I don't handle all of this as well as you. I can't just let things roll off me."

Dad laughed, but it wasn't his laugh. It was calculated. Almost mechanical. "I don't handle it better, Susan. I just hide it deeper."

"Either way, what are we going to *do*? How are we going to fix this?"

There was a long pause, and I thought that was all, but then Dad said, "Maybe we could both focus less on what was taken and more on what was left, because it's pretty awesome."

Mom sniffed. "It *is* awesome. But I can't let go yet. Maybe I'm being selfish, but when Lexi's grown, I want to be able to look her in the eye and tell her we tried everything. That we tried to get it back."

There was a soft strum of chords. "I get that. And I'll help however I can." There were more chords, then a few finger-picked notes from "Here Comes the Sun."

"So, I guess you didn't really burn your arm?" Dad's happy, light tone had returned.

"No. Even half-starved that cat is feisty."

"Yeah . . . Did you really have to butter the whole cat? I mean, couldn't you have just buttered his ear?"

Mom laughed. "You know I can't do anything halfway."

I let out a deep breath and opened my eyes.

The room spun. I felt like I had been plunked down into the cyclone scene in *The Wizard of Oz*. I was lying on Dorothy's bed as her house was swept into the sky. Scenes from everyday life flew past the window. All the pieces of my life were still there, but nothing was in place. I just wanted to make sense of it all.

Something stolen. Something broken. A buttered cat. And Mom, desperate enough to lie and keep secrets. Desperate enough for a devious plan. And now Dad was in on it too?

CHAPTER 30
Age 5, The Year of the Buttered Cat

In the weeks after the overheard confession, I became more and more frustrated with the fact that I had zero control over the pace of my life. I had to wait for things to happen to me, wait for information to blow past. It was all so *passive*.

I thought about Governor White, stranded in a harbor waiting for wind to take his sails so he could go back to England then back to his family in the New World.

I felt like I was sitting in my own harbor waiting for my gust of wind. No wind came.

But here's what did happen: every morning, before my brother and sisters woke up, Dad pulled on oven mitts, wrestled The Cat onto the kitchen table, and together, he and Mom buttered The Cat's ears.

Luke sat at their feet wagging his tail while The Cat hissed and twisted, but Dad held tight. When they were done, the buttered cat leaped from the table, and Luke swooped on him, licking his ears top to bottom. And that little bobcat would transform into mellow mush.

Mom and Dad had no idea they had an audience. I was always up way before the other kids. Mom would drag my beanbag to my TV-viewing spot and plop me in front of *Word Girl*. Of course, all I had to do was arch just right, and I had a clear view of the *real* show in the kitchen.

No more clues about Mom's devious plans or Lou's search blew past, so instead I worked on my gifts. As I lay in bed at night, I tried counting them like they were sheep.

One, memory.

Two, words.

Three, humor.

Four, I don't know.

Five, I don't know.

I repeated the list over and over until I finally fell asleep. I guess I was hoping another gift would jump into the lineup. I wanted an Aha! moment. But the only one I had was that they don't tend to show up when you're looking for them.

I would've been flat-out miserable, except for one thing. The woods around our house had taken on the airy green tinge that meant spring was on its way.

Spring meant there would soon be swinging and sliding and bare feet and ice cream on the porch. And most of all, spring meant my birthday was coming.

One late-March morning, Mom took me, Hannah, and Tucker to the park to do our schoolwork.

In between lessons, we conquered the playground. The three of them took turns hauling me up the steps, over the bridge, and down the slide. I squealed as we zoomed down onto sweet, new mulch.

"Lexi's birthday is coming up," Hannah said. She breathed hard as she handed me back to Mom.

"But mine first!" Tucker said, jumping up and down. "Mine is three days before hers, and I want a party at the movies."

Mom gave Tucker a thumbs up. He pumped his fists and did a victory lap around the playground.

Hannah ignored him. "Know what we should do for Lexi? A friend party!"

I arched and squealed. I only ever had family birthdays, but this year, I had actual friends.

Mom smiled. "I think you're old enough for that. Let's invite Anna and Elle and all your friends from French class. We can decorate the back porch and play party games."

Hannah shook her head. "If we're gonna do this we should do it all the way. How about Monkey Joe's?"

"Mon-key Joe's! Mon-key Joe's!" Tucker chanted.

I stuck out my tongue. I had seen TV commercials for that place. Kids climbing and laughing on a ginormous blow-up playground. Happy, excited faces. Obstacle courses, slides, and bouncy houses.

"I don't know," Mom said. "How can that be fun for Lexi?"

Mom! Seriously? I arched hard and groaned.

"We'll carry her," Hannah said.

"Yeah!" Tucker said. "We just carried her around the playground for an hour."

I stuck out my tongue. *Please, yes! Please?*

Mom stared at me for a long moment. "I'll look into it when we get home."

Hannah picked up my hand and high-fived me.

That afternoon Mom wheeled me up to the table with Haha then disappeared into her office.

Tucker touched letters on Haha's screen then stood back. "Go ahead. Say it."

I hit the top button and Haha announced, "Tucker's birthday is first, and he needs ice cream cake and a Super Mario video game."

"Thanks, Lexi. Do me a favor and keep saying that," Tucker said.

Hannah reached over and also typed something. "Now say that."

I moved the cursor to the top. "Tucker's birthday is first, and he needs deodorant."

I laughed and hit the button twice more.

Haha had lived up to her name, but after nearly two months of daily practice, the top button was still the only one

I could hit every time. My brother and sisters took full advantage and typed in reminders and suggestions for Mom or random insults for each other. I would look at the screen, and Haha would say, "Kasey has a hair appointment at three" or "Hannah is a butthead."

Mom reappeared in the kitchen. "It's all set up! We'll have your party at Monkey Joe's next Friday. It's during home-school hours so it won't be so crowded."

I squealed.

"But *after* my party, right?" Tucker said. "Because my birthday is first."

"Yes," said Mom. "It will be after yours. What do you want for your birthday?"

I looked at Haha. "Tucker's birthday is first, and he needs deodorant."

CHAPTER 31
Age 13, 12½ hours until surgery

I'm standing with Mom at the top of the hospital play structure, staring down a long yellow slide when I hear two
Facebook pings in a row. *Please, let it be them.* I arch and writhe.

"Lexi! I'm going to drop you if you don't hold still."

Dad is stretched out on top of a picnic table. He doesn't sit
up but lifts his arm and waves his phone. "Finish up and we'll
read your messages."

Mom wrestles me into a sit. Thick, dark clouds have rolled
in along with gusty wind. I love how the front side of a summer storm—all wild and swirly—makes me feel like a little kid
again. How its rawness urges me to forget everything ahead
and just do *now*. And in this now, Mom and I are both kids.

Mom pulls the tennis ball from her shorts pocket. Gus
waits, looking up at us. His tail is wagging.

Mom positions the ball on my lap. I twist and flail until I
knock it loose. It bounces down the slide, over Gus, and into
the grass.

He leaps after it, catches it in his mouth, then immediately drops it and lies down on top.

Two pigtailed girls laugh and run toward him.

A lady—maybe their mom—grabs them by the arms. "You can't just run up and pet dogs you don't know."

"It's fine," Dad says. "They can pet him if they want."

Gus isn't wearing his service dog vest, so technically, right now he's just a dog.

The girls wriggle free and slump beside him, rubbing his back. He lifts his chin and smiles.

"His name is Gus," Mom says.

Six eyes find the top of the slide and flicker over me. I pump my arms up and down to wave, but by the look on their faces, it must look like I'm attempting to fly.

"What's wrong with her?" one of the girls asks.

I wait for the stammered apology and clunky retreat. It's usually quick, like an awkward version of the Five-Second Rule. If you drop food on the floor but pick it up fast, you can still eat it. If you grab your kid and run off before I react, their words don't hurt. Science, by the way, has disproved the Five-Second Rule.

The lady flushes but at least she doesn't make a run for it.

"This is Lexi, and she has muscles that work differently from yours," Mom says.

"Can she walk?"

"With help."

"I can walk," one of the girls says. "And run."

Both girls jump up and demonstrate.

"Not everyone is so lucky," the lady says. "You should be thankful for your strong legs."

I want to shout, "I don't want to be you!"

And it's true. I don't want to be them or anyone else. I'm fine with who I am. I *like* who I am. I mean, I get it that I'm different, but why do people assume I hate being me?

I twist to try and catch Mom's gaze. Most days, she'll set the record straight.

Tell them I can be lucky too. That I'm not a worst-case scenario.

But the long day is etched on her face. She gives a weak smile as the lady waves goodbye and chases her girls around the playground.

"Ready?" Mom asks.

She leans back and picks up our feet. We coast to the bottom.

After one more round on the slide, Mom and Dad lift me into my chair. Dad pulls out his phone, and I squeal.

"You have lots of encouraging posts on your last picture. Would you like me to read them to you?"

He's teasing me again. I make a swipe for his phone, but I'm not even close.

"I suppose you want to hear your messages first."

I try for a "yeah," but I'm still out of breath. Instead I stick out my tongue.

"They're from Anna and Elle," he says, and I squeal so loud a couple walking by turn to stare.

I don't care. I flail.

"I'll let you read these in private."

He turns the phone, and a message pops up. I will my eyes to focus on each word.

Hi Lex! Woulda messaged u earlier but Mom banned us from the internet for fighting. Totally Anna's fault. Anyway, miss u. NC is boring without u.

I laugh so hard I can barely breathe. Finally, I recover and point to the phone.

Dad scrolls down to the next message.

NOT my fault. She's just mad cuz I told Mom she was binge-ing HP fanfic when we were told 2 clean our rooms . . . She's right about the boring part. Can't wait till ur back. Did u hang the banner yet?

I laugh hard again, then suddenly, I'm crying. Those two will never change. That's what I love about them. I remember the day I met them. We were at Ms. Joann's for our first-ever

French class. I was having a "bad body day" as my family used to say. I was twisting and arching, and I bet I looked like a sea creature plucked from the ocean. Mom was having a hard time even holding me.

Elle came right up to me, and do you know what she said? She said, "I like your shoes."

That was all. They were old pink Chucks with Gryffindor laces.

Then, Anna picked up my foot so she could get a closer look. I don't know why, but that meant something. Maybe because most kids just looked at me. No one ever touched me.

Mom and Dad are looking at me like I just sprouted a second head. Dad's phone pings again. This one is the text ping.

"Oh! It's Steve Shapiro," Dad says. "He wants to meet us in the hospital chapel at seven."

"Tonight? It's nearly six already. We better get dinner first," says Mom.

I'm not sure what to think. My doctor wants to meet me in the chapel the night before brain surgery. Is this a bad omen?

My scaffolding shifts. I slip a little closer to the edge. I squeeze my rock.

The wind whips over us. The voice is more insistent. *Hurry. Hurry.*

Deep breath in. My story. Breath out.

CHAPTER 32
Age 6, The Year of the Buttered Cat

The next week, Tucker had his birthday party at the movies with ice cream cake and a Super Mario Brothers video game. Finally, Friday came. It was my turn.

At Monkey Joe's, the receptionist showed us to our party room. We had a few minutes before my friends would be there, so Hannah suggested we give the play space a test run.

The inflatables were way bigger than I had imagined. I think they were bigger than Mom had imagined too. She pointed to a purple and yellow slide that towered over us.

"How are you going to get her up there?"

"Like that," Hannah said. She nodded toward a mural of a monkey wrapped around a coconut tree.

Mom and Tucker draped me over Hannah's back. They wrapped my legs around her waist then pulled my arms over her shoulders.

"Okay," Mom said. "Be careful out there."

We climbed onto the first inflatable.

I took a deep breath. This was it. A real-life adventure. I was . . . I was . . . *Princess Leia dodging stormtroopers on a speeder bike?* No. *Harry flying Buckbeak over the Hogwarts lake?* No.

I had been so busy hanging out with new friends I hadn't visited my old ones in weeks. I guess I was a little rusty.

C'mon. Choose . . . Yes! Got it!

I hummed the *Indiana Jones* theme song in my head as we squeezed through a forest of soft columns and crawled up and over yellow hills. When Hannah wobbled, I could feel Tucker's hand pressed on my back. Finally, we reached a purple mountain with a built-in ladder.

Hannah breathed hard. "If we can make it to the top, there's a slide on the other side. Ready?"

Tongue out.

"Eww, you licked my neck." She scrunched her shoulders. "Sometimes I wish you could just *say* yes."

I stuck out my tongue again, but *not* to say yes.

We began to climb. Hannah leaned close to the ladder, gripping the side with one hand and squeezing my hands with the other. Tucker's hand was firm on my back. Part way up we stopped. Hannah leaned in, panting.

I loosened my grip a bit, looked down, and learned something new about myself. I was afraid of heights. My breathing sped up to match Hannah's. I arched. Tucker pushed harder.

"Lexi, take a deep breath and count to five," Hannah said.

I breathed in.

One, two, three, four, five.

Nothing.

One, two, three, four, five.

Nothing.

I arched more.

"Lexi! Count something. Anything! Count sheep or pretzels or whatever. Just count!"

I breathed in again, and this time the list I had repeated so many times leaped into my brain:

One, memory.

Two, words.

Three, humor.

Four, I don't know.

Five, I don't know.

One, memory.

Two, words.

Three, humor.

Four, I don't know.

Five, I don't know.

I don't know.

I. Don't. Know.

I don't know if there is a four or a five . . .

There. I had said it—or at least thought it.

I think it's probably common for a rock climber, looking down from a mountain face, to question the most basic truths of her life. For me, clinging to my sister's back ten feet up an inflatable mountain was gonna have to do.

I buried my face in Hannah's hair.

What if that's it? What if there is no four? Or five?

I thought back to Crazy Mr. Bean's prophecy: "This child will have five gifts. Give or take a few . . . I can't be absolutely sure of the number."

All this time I've been looking for more, but what if . . . what if this is all?

We were moving again. My breaths continued in heaves.

And if there isn't a four, and there isn't a five, then . . . where is my body? Why hasn't it come?

Hannah rolled onto the top platform. I let go of her neck, and Tucker collapsed beside me. For a long moment, the three of us lay there, panting.

"You know what, Lexi?" Hannah said. "You're a lot heavier than you look."

Tucker picked me up so we could see how high we were. Below, Mom paced, then spotted us and waved.

We had made it! Today I would blow out six candles on my cake and make a wish for whatever I wanted. I could wish for more gifts, or for my body to come in, or to ride a hippogriff, and *yes!* I wanted all of that. But right in that moment, what I wanted more than anything was to always have my friends and family there for me.

"Are you ready to slide down?" Hannah asked.

Tongue out.

Hannah plopped me on to Tucker's lap. She gave him a push from behind, and we zoomed to the bottom.

Mom picked me up and pointed to the entrance where Anna and Elle and the rest of my friends from French class were waiting.

For the next hour, Hannah and Tucker led us all on more expeditions, with me clinging to Hannah's back, and then, when she was too tired, to Tucker's back, until Mom called us into our party room.

Everyone drank juice boxes and sang "Happy Birthday to You" as Mom lit the candles on my cake. She plucked a candle from the middle and held it up.

"Make a wish!" she said.

And I did. Together, we all blew out my candle.

CHAPTER 33
Age 6, The Year of the Buttered Cat

Have you ever tried to leash a cat? Once, when The Cat disappeared, Tucker thought he found him prowling around a neighbor's yard. We later found out *that* gray cat lived there, but Tucker didn't know it. He was sure it was The Cat, and he tried to bring him home by slipping Luke's leash around his neck. There was scratching and biting (from the cat) as well as earsplitting screeches (from Tucker *and* the cat). Tucker finally let him go and decided this: You can put a leash around a cat's neck, make kissy sounds, and bribe him with treats, but if that cat doesn't want to come with you, that cat isn't coming with you.

From that day on, when anyone in our family has tried to force something in a direction it doesn't want to go, we've called that "leashing the cat."

Kali attempting to straighten her thick, curly hair during our North Carolina summers was leashing the cat.

Mom instructing Tucker to sit right side up and finish his math assignments was leashing the cat.

And in the weeks following my birthday party, persuading my brain to think about gifts was also leashing the cat. I had worked so long and hard on my gift search that I just couldn't go there anymore.

The deadline was still nearly four months away. Plenty of time. Maybe it wouldn't hurt to take a little break. After all, my third gift had appeared when I was least expecting it.

The freedom was amazing. For the first time in nearly a year I didn't pick apart each moment like a buzzard on roadkill.

Every morning, I had a rubberneck view of the buttering of The Cat. Dad in his oven mitts held down a wriggling, raging fireball. Mom, the fencer, *en garde* with her buttered spatula, lunged forward. The Cat blocked jab after jab until Mom faked right, swung left, and landed a greasy hit.

As I watched, I practiced my lightsaber skills at the Jedi Academy or my wand technique at Hogwarts.

I also attended my end-of-school French celebration at the community center of Ms. Joann's church. Mom wheeled me around the stage while I played the part of a magical tree in our class play. After that, Ms. Joann presented me with a fourth-place ribbon for the National French Exam. Anna and Elle placed too, so Mom and Ms. Trejo took about a million pictures of us with our ribbons. Before we left, there were hugs and promises for lots of summer get-togethers. Avery and

Marc even dragged their parents over to hear my Chewbacca impression.

A week later we had the spring festival at Mitey Riders. My whole family watched as I rode around the rink with my team and received my trophy.

It was during these public events that I discovered one of life's simple pleasures: goosing people who stood too close to my wheelchair. It started innocently enough. At the end of the French program, everyone had rushed the exit at once. Kasey was pushing my chair, and we found ourselves stuck in a thick crowd.

I told my arms to not move, so *obviously* they flew out. Each hand grabbed something. That something turned out to be two butts. The owners of those butts jumped and turned to look at me.

Kasey pulled my arms in and apologized. The two people smiled and shuffled out of reach. In no time, two more victims came within striking distance. Out flew the arms.

I discovered that if I timed it just right, my hands could do a quick pinch and release. My victim would look around, then turn back with a confused expression like they had imagined it all. Kasey pretended not to notice, but I heard her make a little laugh-snort. By the time we reached the exit, I'd managed to goose six people.

The following week at the Mitey Riders finale, Mom was pushing my chair. She was so distracted she didn't even notice what my hands were up to. All in all, I goosed eight people that day, and I was pretty sure no one suspected me.

And so began my career as a bandit butt pincher. I kept a running tally in my head. My goal each day was to add to my total, if not break my Mitey Riders record. It was the first time I could make a reliable, repeatable movement with more than one muscle, and it was fantastic.

At this rate, by fall I could probably learn how to swipe wallets and cell phones. Maybe I'd make the switch from superhero to villain. The possibilities were endless. Yep, my summer of go-with-the-flow was shaping up to be amazing.

CHAPTER 34
Age 13, 11½ hours until surgery

We're back in the hospital cafeteria. Before me is a feast of macaroni and cheese, green beans, mashed potatoes, a yogurt parfait, and an ice cream sandwich. I don't know if I can eat it all, but I'm gonna try.

This is the last solid food I'll have for days. Mom and Dad didn't blink at my food choices.

This whole day has hinged on *lasts*. My last play time with Gus. Last coast down the slide. After my last meal, I'll brush my teeth, and Mom will put me in bed for the last time.

All day, I've built a wall, brick by brick, one last event at a time. It's a wall between before and after. On the other side lies the rest of my life. A life with talking, singing, and shouting? Or a life where I struggle to remember who I am or where I've been?

At that thought, my appetite vanishes.

"Lexi, you have to eat," Mom says. "You know this is the last chance you'll have for . . . for a while."

Mom and Dad have tried hard not to talk about lasts. I wonder if their before and after looks different from mine. From the worry etched on their faces all day, I think it does. Suddenly, I'm overcome with shame for putting them through this again.

I'm sorry. I can't think of anything more meaningful or soothing.

What I really want right now is a good cry, but instead I open my mouth and eat. For Mom. As if a few bites of mac 'n' cheese can make up for all *this*.

Finally, Dad puts our trays on the service line, and we head to the hospital chapel.

Mom rolls me inside, and my breath catches a little. This is not what I was expecting. The chapel is two stories, paneled top to bottom in pale wood. One side is dominated by a screen carved with a pattern that looks like waves or pebbles or maybe waves of pebbles.

Despite the storm clouds outside, ceiling-to-floor windows flood the chapel with the sort of light that makes me feel like I'm standing in a field. Beyond the glass, I see a ceramic fountain and a garden in full bloom.

But it's the music that really takes my breath away. Someone is playing my favorite Beatles song—"Blackbird"— on a baby grand piano, and the thick, rich chords bring the room to life. I sing along in my head.

The music stops and Steve rises at the piano bench. He's wearing cargo shorts and Birkenstocks. "You made it!"

Mom and Dad are spinning slowly, like two little kids. They don't answer.

"Pretty cool, isn't it?" he asks.

"Gorgeous," Mom answers. "I've never seen a hospital chapel like this."

Truth. The whole place is bright and hopeful—so different from the tiny dark chapels we've rolled past in other hospitals. And I do mean rolled *past.* We've never, ever wanted to go inside one of those. Mom always says they feel like death, waiting.

Steve hands Dad a guitar. "I borrowed it from the chaplain. Probably needs tuning."

Dad plucks strings and turns pegs. I realize it's the first time I've seen him smile—really smile—since morning. He pulls up a chair next to the piano, and when the music starts, the room springs back to life.

Mom sees me tapping a finger. She takes me from my wheelchair, and right there in the hospital chapel, I dance. Gus jumps up and tries to dance too. We all laugh.

We move from Beatles to John Coltrane to Thelonious Monk. When Mom can't hold me on my feet any longer, we lie on our backs and watch the lights that hang from the arched ceiling like individual stars.

"Thanks, Steve. That's exactly what we needed tonight," Dad says as he puts the guitar back in its case.

"We have different hats to wear tomorrow, and it'll be a long day," Steve says.

I want to drink in all this happiness and contentment and hopefulness so I can remember it later. Remember it tomorrow.

We roll back out into the noise and fluorescent lights, and the good vibes start to leak out of me. I close my eyes to trap them inside.

Deep breath in. My story. Breath out.

CHAPTER 35
Age 6, The Year of the Buttered Cat

That year, summer burst into Charlotte like the fire-breathing dragon from the vaults at Gringotts. I cooled off at the pool, listened to books, and played loads of Hangman, Mad Libs, and hide-and-seek. But it was the three things I *didn't* do that defined my summer.

1. I didn't search for gifts.
2. I didn't find any gifts.
3. I didn't hang out with Anna and Elle. Not even once.

And here's the crazy thing: even though I could feel my deadline closing in, could hear that ticking clock growing louder and louder, the one that bothered me the most was number three.

Mom said that sometimes summers are just *like* that—you get out of your old routine and into a new one. Things get busy. You forget.

Well, maybe Mom forgot. Maybe Ms. Trejo forgot. I never forgot. *Obviously.*

The thing about summer is that absolutely nothing can happen for days or even weeks, then *bam!* Everything happens all in one day.

Monday, July 28, turned out to be one of those *bam!* days.

I should back up. It actually *started* the night before. Mom had said that our loaner period was up and that we had to return Haha to the Center on Monday.

Dad took her from her spot at the kitchen table and packed her in a box with a bubble wrap blanket.

He taped the box shut and said, "I'm gonna miss this one, but she's a loaner so she has to go back." Then, like a lightbulb had just clicked on in his brain, he added, "And she'll also enjoy some me-time in her box tonight."

Everyone groaned. I was spelling with Mom, so I reached for my letters.

DAD! That's loner. No A.

Dad smacked his forehead.

Mom said, "So, the big question is, do you want Celeste to order you one of your own? One for keeps?"

I pushed letters around on my board but didn't answer.

The crazy thing was, I was gonna miss Haha too. She had been an important part of some awesome games and pranks. She had totally lived up to her name. But I still hated computerized speech with a burning passion. The first day I set eyes on Haha at the Center, I had made a list in my head of all the reasons why I hated her. Those hadn't changed.

I wanted a *real* voice, one with tone and inflections—a voice that sounded like *me*, not like a computer.

I wanted a voice that didn't take *forever* to say what I wanted.

Most of all, I wanted to talk the way everyone else on the planet was talking. Was that too much to ask?

But right then, I really didn't want to hear that answer. Instead, I spelled, **What kind of underwear does Spider-Man wear?**

Dad said, "Definitely tighty whiteys."

Tucker said, "None! He goes commando."

Mom took my hint and didn't say anything.

So, *bam!* day, Monday, July 28, started with me sitting in my car seat and Haha the loaner, or loner, resting in her box on the front seat.

I didn't want to look at her or think about her. Instead, I stared at one of my stickers that had started to peel away from the ceiling. It had a pink heart in the middle that said, *Be Mine*. I practiced my telepathy.

C'mon. Fall off. You know you want to. If you fall, Tucker will sit on you, and you'll stick to his butt.

The sticker curled in the midsummer humidity. I thought of Tucker walking around with *Be Mine* stuck to his shorts.

That's it. A little more. You can do it.

Mom braked for a light. The sticker fluttered to the seat beside me. I squealed. My first telepathic success.

"What's up, Buttercup?" Celeste asked as we rolled in at the Center.

I uncurled my index finger.

"Is that my device in there?"

Tongue out.

"Your mom says you aren't sure if you want one. Is that right?"

Tongue out.

Celeste pulled up a chair and sat next to me. "I have a surprise. Do you want to know what it is?"

She didn't wait for my answer. She picked up a letter from her desk.

"Dear Ms. Helling, Thank you for your recent nomination of Lexi Haas for the North Carolina Assistive Technology Award of Excellence. As you know, this award recognizes an individual for their accomplishments in the use of assistive technology. We're delighted to inform you that Ms. Haas has been selected as the winner of this year's award, which will be presented at our annual conference next month."

Celeste looked up and smiled. I stared at her, waiting for the punchline. No one in their right mind would give *me* an award for accomplishments in assistive technology.

Instead, she continued to read. "Please inform Ms. Haas she's been selected so she can prepare a short acceptance speech."

I arched and grimaced. This was crazy. Why wasn't Mom objecting? She knew this was a joke.

"Hold up, Buttercup. It's not like you have to write a Gettysburg Address. Two or three sentences will be fine. If you want, you can just write it on your cookie sheet. We can decide about the device later."

I frowned.

"Now don't get too excited. I think you may be the youngest person ever to win."

On the ride home, I stared at the bare spot on the ceiling where *Be Mine* had been stuck. The outline was still visible, probably because it had been stuck to that same spot for over three years.

I remembered the day when the dental hygienist held it out and said, "This was for being such a sweet, helpful girl today during your cleaning!"

Mom had quietly accepted my reward. She added it to my collection when we got to the van, but the truth was, I had bit the dentist during my exam. Twice. I hadn't done it on purpose, but even at three years old, I knew "sweet" and "helpful" were not the words that were going into my chart that day.

And next to the empty spot was Dora the Explorer shouting, *"Hola!"* I got that one last year at the orthopedist's office even though I had kicked the radiology technician right between his legs during my hip X-rays. Again, unintentional, but did I mention it was *right* between his legs? The receptionist presented me with the sticker and told me how cooperative I had been.

And above my window was the Hulk sticker from the pediatrician. That day I had whacked a needle from the nurse's hand every time he got within poking distance.

Yeah, that one was intentional.

I sighed. I wanted a real award. It felt so good claiming my French ribbon because I knew I had earned it. That's the kind of recognition I wanted.

"Guess who's receiving the Award of Excellence at the assistive technology conference next month?" Mom asked as she rolled me into the house.

"Me!" Tucker stood on the coffee table and raised his arms in victory.

Hannah pushed him, and he fell backwards onto the couch.

"Is an 'assistive technology conference' really a thing?" Kasey called from the kitchen.

I laughed. Mom stiffened.

"Lexi was chosen for this award, and we should be really

happy for her. In fact . . ." She paused. "In fact, we're going out to dinner tonight to celebrate."

That got everyone's attention.

"That sounds great! How about Mexican, Lexi?" Kali asked.

Mom cleared her throat.

"That's great about the award," Kali added.

"She's even giving an acceptance speech," Mom said.

"That's cool! Do you know what you're gonna say?" asked Hannah.

Ggguuhhh. I arched and grimaced.

"Cool your jets, Lex," Kali said. "Words are your thing. I'm sure this speech will practically write itself."

"And you don't even have to write it on the device," said Mom. "You can spell it on your cookie sheet, and we'll type it into Haha for the ceremony."

I sighed. This whole thing was a sham. Honored for accomplishments in assistive technology, but someone else would type my speech into the device. *Geez*. Still, I knew there was no way I was getting out of this.

The rest of the afternoon I tried to think of what I might say, but it was leashing the cat. I had never had trouble putting words together before, but now all I could think of was, *"I'm sure this speech will practically write itself."*

Mom put me on my bed to rest. The midafternoon sun glinted off my Mitey Riders trophy. My *participation* trophy.

My celebration dinner at El Paso turned out to be just the distraction I needed. The thick, noisy crowd was the perfect setup for a heist, and from my wheelchair I stole butt pinches like a pro.

Midway through dinner, I looked around the restaurant, soaking up music and clatter and bustle. Back in the far corner, something caught my eye. I leaned towards it, staring. Could it really be? I leaned more. It was! Anna and Elle and all the kids from French class were *here* eating dinner. Together. Without me.

Elle shot a spitball through her straw at McRae, who laughed and slapped her arm. The others were all there too—*even* Avery and Marc. All of them were laughing. Having fun. Without me. Why hadn't they invited me?

As soon as I asked, the answer popped in my head. *Sides. Sometimes it's hard to be on the other side too.*

I knew how it was—everyone who could walk, everyone who could talk, everyone who could *everything* on one side. Me on the other. Yeah? Well, it didn't *look* that hard to be on the other side. I watched Anna lean in and whisper to Martine.

Suddenly, I wanted to go. Needed to get out of there. I screeched and arched.

"Lexi, what's *wrong* with you?" Mom asked. "Everyone's still eating."

What's wrong with you? The question stung like an unexpected slap. I started to cry.

"Lexi, I'm sorry. I didn't mean—"

She hugged me until I quieted.

She looked around the restaurant. Her expression turned cold.

"Oh . . . I see. Well, I'm going over to say hi. At least let them know we saw them."

Ggguuhhh. My eyes pleaded with her.

"No? Are you sure?"

Tongue out. Sometimes, moms only make things worse. I just wanted to *go.*

"Lexi's hot so I'm gonna take her outside," Mom said. "Just meet us by the van when you're done."

We wheeled around the parking lot, watching the last bit of sun drop behind the skyline. When my French class friends came out, laughing and punching each other, Mom rolled me around to the other side of the building.

"Oh, look at these. Hybrid Tea Roses!"

We rolled up to a hedge of creamy lavender flowers. She plucked one and breathed in deep, then held it under my nose. It was fresh and delicate and so *familiar.* Images of our garden in Virginia popped into my head—Mom, with me on her hip, standing in front of a bush that looked exactly like this one.

"Some of my favorite flowers," she said. "When we lived in Virginia, I grew five different kinds. Boy, did I have to baby them—the feeding, the pruning! And in winter I'd be out in the freezing cold covering them up, so they wouldn't die back to the ground. By spring, I'd swear that I was done with them, that I'd plant something *easier*. Then the branches would suddenly green up. By summer, these blossoms would pop, and you could smell them a mile away. I'd come in from the garden with my hands ripped to pieces from the thorns, but I couldn't help myself."

She took another deep breath.

I smiled. Mom hardly ever talked about Virginia anymore. I wanted to hear more. *Tell me about the garden. And the swing set. And . . . all of it.*

"There you are!" Dad called to us. "We've been looking all over for you."

"We're just admiring the flowers," Mom said.

Dad hugged her and she swallowed hard. We walked back toward the van.

"This was a lot better than the last time we went out to eat," Tucker said. "Remember Crazy Mr. Bean?"

Hannah laughed. "I forgot all about that!"

In all the commotion of the day, I had forgotten too. July 28. My five-gift prophecy had been exactly one year ago.

I thought back to the excitement and anticipation I had felt in *that* parking lot. The prophecy had been a promise of a future I wanted so badly to understand, but instead it had brought more questions than answers. A full year later, I still didn't know what my gifts were, when my body was coming in, or why it was all taking so long. And to top it off, now I had no friends.

I have no body and nobody.

CHAPTER 36
Age 6, The Year of the Buttered Cat

We drove home from El Paso in silence. Dad pulled into our driveway, and Mom gasped.

"What?" Dad asked.

"Look!"

She pointed to a shadowy area of our front yard. A streetlamp cast soft light over three enormous cats surrounding a smaller, gray figure. That center figure was puffed up and hissing.

"Territory fight!" Kali jumped from the van and ran toward the fight, but two of the cats turned toward her and hissed. She backed away. "Get a broom or something!"

Mom opened the back door, and Luke flew past her. He ran toward the brawl, growling and barking. The three cats bolted for the woods.

The Cat figure-eighted Luke's legs and purred. Luke sniffed him then barked twice as if to say, "And stay out!"

He trotted to the house, The Cat close behind.

Inside, everyone was talking at once.

"Where did those cats come from?"

"They were huge!"

"I've never seen them around here before."

Dad looked at Mom. "You haven't been—"

"Of course not! What kind of cat café do you think I'm running here?"

I laughed, picturing a sign hanging at our front door. *Cat ears buttered here daily.*

"What do you mean by cat café?" Kasey asked.

Mom sighed. She and Dad told the whole story of the buttered cat.

Hannah and Kasey stared at them, hands over mouths.

"So, this cat buttering craziness has to stop," Kali said. "Luke must be imprinting his scent on The Cat, and it's seriously pissing off the neighborhood. Plus, all that fat is bad for Luke. It can give him pancreatitis, you know."

Dad took a deep breath and nodded slowly. Mom sat down at the table, covered her face, and began to cry.

"I'm so confused!" Tucker said. "You hate cats!"

Dad put his arm around Mom. "This has nothing to do with cats."

I tried to send her a telepathic message. *My body is coming. Soon! It will be here as soon as I find my gifts.* But the message was weak and staticky, like a cell phone moving too far from a tower.

Dad picked up an envelope from a pile of mail on the counter. "When did this come?"

"Just now," Hannah said. "I brought it from the mailbox after we chased off the cats."

Dad turned it over. The familiar gold lettering flashed at the top. He ripped it open, and his eyes darted back and forth over the paper.

"Why? What is it?" Kali asked.

Dad ignored her. For a minute, he just stood there staring into the paper.

Finally, he let out a deep breath and pushed the letter toward Mom. "Well, you were right. Lou can't help us. It's over."

"Help us what?" Kasey asked.

Mom scanned the letter. "It's nothing." She squeezed Dad's hand. "Nothing we didn't already know."

I knew, and for the first time, there was no satisfaction in being the only one. *He can't help me. He can't help me find my missing things.*

I swallowed hard. Now I was completely on my own. My deadline was just weeks away. Did it even matter?

The rest of that week was quiet. Creepy quiet. Even at night when I lay in bed, no music seeped in through my walls. Not one note.

Mom kept asking me if I wanted her to call Ms. Trejo. She said she was sure it was all a misunderstanding, but I wouldn't let her. I squeezed my imaginary rock. The familiar rough edges now felt sharp and prickly.

No thank you.

Being my friend, being on my side, was hard. I got that. I took work. *Obviously* too much work.

Every afternoon, Mom gathered me on her lap and tried to get me to work on my speech, but no words came. The letters stayed lined up at the top of my cookie sheet, like an army of soldiers waiting to be called into battle.

That whole week, I didn't spell *anything*. What good were words? I didn't have anyone I wanted to talk to or anything I needed to say.

Instead, I stared at the blank sheet until Spider-Man or the Hulk or Luke and Leia showed up and swept me off on an adventure. Harry, Ron, and Hermione always tried to tag along, but I hit them with the Obliviate Charm and told them to get lost. *Obviously.*

On Saturday, when Mom pulled me onto her lap, there was a message waiting for me. **Hi Lexi. This is your cookie sheet. I miss you. Please tell me something.**

I stared at the words.

Finally, Mom wrote, **Pretty please?**

I sighed and pulled down letters. **My dog eats cheese, shoes, and library books. But mostly string cheese, sneakers, and books about cats.**

Mom snorted, and I admit it was good to at least hear one of my parents laugh again.

She wrote, **Spider-Man wears Hulk underwear.**

Ggguuhhh.

I reached forward. **Spider-Man wears Green Goblin underwear. So he can sit on him. That is all.**

The next day, at 3 p.m., Mom pulled me onto her hip. "C'mon, Lex, we have work to do."

I thought we were going to have another stare down with my cookie sheet, but instead, she stood with me at the bottom of the stairs and shouted, "*SNL!*"

I squealed with both relief and excitement.

Upstairs, a door creaked open.

"So . . . we're doing this?" Kali asked, leaning over the railing.

Mom nodded. I stuck out my tongue.

One by one, the kids filtered down the stairs and into the den. Dad was last, shaking his head and smiling sheepishly. "You know, I forgot to record it last night."

"What? You think I can't work the DVR?" Mom asked. She tossed him the remote. "Well, c'mon. It's not gonna play itself."

Dad flopped onto the couch and took me from Mom. He folded my legs crisscross applesauce and wrapped his arms tight around my chest. His breathing slowed to match mine, and he rested his head on my shoulder. We sat like that through the whole show.

CHAPTER 37
Age 13, 8½ hours until surgery

As we roll back to the Ronald McDonald House for the last time, it begins to rain, little shards of glass against my face. Mom and Dad break into a jog. We roll under the awning in front of the house just as the sky opens. Water quickly overwhelms the gutters and downspouts. Thunder crashes much too close. Safe and dry, we watch the fury, and I think, *See, I'm lucky.*

Inside, the front desk is empty. Normally, someone is here to greet us no matter what time we roll in or out, but the receptionist must have run upstairs to deliver a blanket or fix a thermostat.

We stop by the kitchen where leftovers from dinner lay covered on the counter, ready for stragglers from the hospital.

"You barely touched your dinner. Want a snack?" Mom asks.

I'm not really hungry, but I think Mom might need the distraction. I stick out my tongue. She peels back the foil.

"Smoked chicken," she announces. "Smells good."

I eat slowly and look around the deserted kitchen. *Where is everyone?* Normally, other families hang around after dinner to chat and catch up, but I guess everyone turned in early tonight.

We take my last elevator ride up to our room and roll through the door one last time. Gus stands over his bowl, waiting for his last dinner.

We are completely silent. Even Gus, who usually whimpers impatiently for his food, has nothing to say.

I sit in my chair and admire the boring old *sameness* of our evening routine. Brush teeth, change into pajamas, feed the dog.

A mechanical shriek pierces the room. Dad, his toothbrush dangling from his foaming mouth, throws open the door and finds the hallway echoing with the relentless, pulsating scream of an alarm.

Another wail joins the first. This one is coming from outside. With each passing moment, it grows louder and closer.

Mom yanks open the blinds and stares into the driving, night rain.

"Fire trucks!"

Dad hops around the room on one foot, pulling on tennis shoes as he grabs Gus's leash.

Mom rolls me out into the hall. We're met with families streaming toward the stairway in their pajamas. Firefighters, dressed in full-on protective gear, are marching down the hall, banging on doors. One even has a shovel. A shovel!

"Everyone downstairs," he commands.

Dad pushes the elevator button.

"Sir! You cannot use the elevator!" shovel-guy shouts.

"But my kid is in a wheelchair!"

"You'll have to use the stairs. Do you need help?"

Ggguuhhh. Please don't let shovel-guy pick me up!

Dad shakes his head, heaves me onto his shoulder, and we work our way down the stairs with Mom and Gus right behind us.

Downstairs, families are gathered by the entrance, stuck between a fierce thunderstorm on the outside and a potential fire on the inside.

Mom pulls up a chair, and Dad swings me down to her lap.

"It's a good thing you're a lightweight, kiddo." He stretches out his back and smiles.

After about a half hour, the firefighters file down the stairs.

"All clear," shovel-guy announces. "It was a minor incident on the third floor."

Families begin to filter back toward the stairway.

"Good luck tomorrow!" Eddie's mom says.

"It's tomorrow?" the lady behind her says, wide-eyed.

Mom nods, and the lady gives her a hug. The man behind her clasps Dad on the shoulder and fist bumps me. As families file back upstairs, they stop for a high five, a hug, or a fist bump.

Katy, her thin frame draped in Hello Kitty pajamas, smiles and says, "You've got this."

I try to fist bump her but miss by a mile.

Finally, it's just us, alone in the lobby.

"I guess we can take the elevator back up. Want me to take her?" Dad asks.

Mom stands up with me, still cradled like a baby in her arms. "No, I've got this."

And together, we make one last trip upstairs.

Deep breath in. My story. Breath out.

CHAPTER 38
Age 6, The Year of the Buttered Cat

Sunday night, notes from Dad's guitar finally filtered through my wall again. It was a jazz tune I had never heard before, but the notes wrapped around me like a warm familiar blanket. Had it really been a week since we both discovered we had been dumped?

I was still miserable, but knowing Dad was getting back to normal made me a less uneasy.

The next day, when Mom sat down with me to spell, my board read, **Speeches sometimes start with, "Good morning! I am . . ."**

Geez. She was *not* gonna let this go. I added my words to hers.

. . . the Lorax. I speak for the trees.

"Dr. Seuss! Nice!" Mom said, undiscouraged. "Quotes are great but be sure and give credit to the author."

She wrote, **Where do you think assistive technology will take you?**

I reached down again.

"I just know before this is over, I'm gonna need a whole lot of serious therapy."—Donkey, from Shrek

Mom read it twice, first the regular way then again in her best Donkey voice, which was terrible.

"Mom! No. Just No," Hannah said, poking her head into the den. "You will ruin that movie for all of us."

"Do you want to give this a shot?"

"Doing *Shrek* impressions? No thanks!" Hannah flopped onto the couch.

"I mean working with Lexi on her speech. I'm clearly not helping." Mom stood up and stretched.

Hannah shrugged. "I'll give it a try."

She sat behind me and pulled over the cookie sheet. "Let's see what you have so far."

I glanced down.

"Seriously? That's it? Haven't you been working on this for like a week?"

I arched and screeched.

"Okay, okay, no big deal. It sounds like you have writer's block."

Writer's Block? That sounded serious and official. I spelled, **Do I need a doctor?**

Hannah snorted. "It's not a disease. It means you're having trouble getting your thoughts on paper. It happens to me all the time. Trust me, you need a change of scenery. Are you up for something different?"

Tongue out.

"Wait here," she said, and she ran out of the room.

In a few minutes, she returned and heaved me onto her shoulder.

"Time for a tea party."

Hannah had spread a blanket on the floor of my room. On top were three toys and my tea set.

"Welcome to your Assistive Technology Q&A," she said.

She pointed to a Princess Leia action figure who was holding a black blaster and straddling a pink plastic teacup.

"Lexi, you already know Celeste," she said. "But did you know on weekends she wears a tunic and hangs out at the firing range?"

I laughed.

She pointed to Mrs. Potato Head and my stuffed owl. "And these ladies are Lois and Toots from the award selection committee. I thought you'd like to ask them some questions."

She folded me onto her lap and pulled over my cookie sheet.

I spelled, **Why me? I have no AT accomplishments**.

"Celeste, Lexi wants to know why you nominated her for this award," Hannah said.

She picked up the Princess Leia doll and turned her to face me. "Well, Buttercup, accomplishments aren't just the feathers in your cap, they're also the birds you meet along the way."

Ggguuhhh. Accomplishments *are* the feathers in your cap. *Obviously.*

"No, I'm serious," Celeste continued. "AT isn't about a destination, like Cleveland or Atlanta. It's the collection of road maps and cheap souvenirs and even the argument you have in the back seat because your brother won't move over when he is clearly in your space . . ."

The blaster flew from Celeste's hand, landing in my teacup. We both laughed.

"Buttercup, I nominated you because you have the biggest collection of cheesy road-trip souvenirs I've ever seen—and you're only six. Now excuse me, I need to find my blaster. Speaking of cheesy, is that cheesy bread over there?"

Kasey appeared in the doorway. "What are you guys doing?"

"We're having a tea party," Hannah said. "A *private* tea party."

Kasey jumped onto my bed and curled up.

Hannah sighed. "We're working on Lexi's award speech. She was a little stuck so we're trying to get ideas flowing."

"Good idea. Is it working?"

Ggguuhhh.

"The problem is that she doesn't think she has accomplishments in Assistive Technology."

Kasey sat up. "Seriously, Lex? You've been using that thing since you were a baby. Don't you think that's an accomplishment?"

I spelled, **This isn't technology. It's a cookie sheet. AT is Haha.**

Kasey shook her head. "Haha is *high-tech* assistive technology, but AT isn't just that." She typed something into her phone. "This says AT can be anything that helps deal with a problem caused by a disability. If you think about it that way, even my glasses can be AT. Your cookie sheet definitely counts. Now, are you gonna offer me tea or not?"

After that, every afternoon I sat down with Hannah to work on my speech. It was slow going so whenever I got stuck, she would pull out Celeste, Lois, and Toots and let me ask them questions. It was a good thing I had nearly a month, because it took that long to finish.

The Monday before the ceremony Celeste brought Haha to the house. Kasey typed in my speech, and I practiced activating the top button until I was sure I could do it at the presentation. It was a little weird hearing my words come to life. It was like stepping back and seeing for the first time an entire house I had built brick by brick with my own hands. The house was tiny and plain, but it was mine.

"Pretty cool, Lex," Kasey said. "You're an author!"

An *author*? Yes! Kasey was right. Somewhere in the last month, I had stopped spelling and started writing. I let that sink in. *Lexi Haas, author.*

"So, I found this sound file on the internet and thought you'd like it," Kasey said.

She showed me a new button she had added to Haha. When I activated it, I nearly jumped out of my wheelchair. The perfect ending.

"Well, I think you're ready!" Hannah said. She shook my hand. "It's been nice working with you."

Ggguuhhh.

"No?"

I pointed to my cookie sheet. There was something else that Lexi Haas, author, needed to say.

Hannah put the cookie sheet on my lap and held my wrist. I wrote, **I need to read a letter and write a letter.**

CHAPTER 39
Age 6, The Year of the Buttered Cat

Surprisingly, neither Kasey nor Hannah gave any pushback to stealing Dad's letter. If it really *was* about me, Kasey pointed out, I had a right to read it.

Later that afternoon, when Mom took Tucker to a dentist appointment, Kasey slipped into Mom's office. A few minutes later, she returned, envelope in hand. The gold lettering shimmered as she held it up.

"Okay, Lexi, remember: This never happened."

"Never happened," agreed Hannah. She waved her hand. "Now hurry up before someone sees us."

Kasey unfolded the letter and held it up for me to see. Hannah ran a finger under each word:

Dear Ken and Susan,

As much as it pains me to report this, my investigation has been unable to uncover additional information regarding the missing records. I must therefore close this case without offering further representation.

Ken, I will personally bring Lexi's records by your office next week. At that time, I would be happy to answer any additional questions you may have. I'm sorry I couldn't provide you with a more satisfying outcome.

Sincerely,

Lou

Louisa Lattimore, J.D.

For a second I stared at the letter, just like Dad had the night it arrived. I tried to wrap my head around the whole thing at once. My missing evidence was just missing records? Records of what? And Lou Lattimore was a woman! No wonder Anna and Elle couldn't find her online.

Hannah and Kasey looked at me wide-eyed.

"It looks like Mom and Dad had some legal thing going," Kasey finally said. She pointed to the gold letterhead: *Lattimore and Goldmann, Attorneys at Law.*

No! Lou Lattimore was a superhero. What the heck was I supposed to do with a lawyer?

"You know, we could ask Mom about it," Hannah said.

Ggguuhhh.

"Are you insane?" Kasey squeaked. "If she knew we were snooping through her stuff we'd be grounded for a year. We have to make a pact. No one tells. Got it?"

I stuck out my tongue. Hannah nodded. It didn't really matter. Superhero or lawyer, Lou couldn't help.

Kasey stuffed the letter back in the envelope and slipped back into Mom's office.

When she returned, she held up her hands. "There. Mission accomplished. Now, didn't you say you had a letter to *write*?"

Friday morning, all seven of us loaded into the van for the nearly three-hour drive to Raleigh for the assistive technology conference where I would receive my award. The meeting was at a fancy hotel, so the trip started with Mom's standard speech about how we were all going to behave like civilized people.

At the end, her eyes settled on Tucker. He threw up his hands and said, "Why do you always look at *me*?"

We stopped for gas, and everyone got out to stretch. I looked out the window at Tucker, who was swinging what I thought was an imaginary lightsaber in the parking lot. My arms tingled. I jumped into battle with him. Together, we took out four stormtroopers who were headed back to the Death Star with their Slurpees.

Mom leaned inside the van. "You okay? You were squealing."

She extended my legs one at a time, then rubbed my hamstrings and calves.

"We're nearly there. Excited?"

Ggguuhhh.

"Nervous?"

Tongue out.

She smiled. "I'll be with you the whole time. Plus, Celeste said they're saving the front row for us. When you look up, you'll see people you know."

That thought relaxed me until Dad pulled into the hotel parking lot. My nerves returned, worse than ever. What if my eyes couldn't find the button on Haha? I pictured myself on stage, my head cranked hard to one side, and everyone laughing.

In the lobby, a woman strode toward me, her arms spread wide, "Buttercup!"

I shrieked.

Celeste led us back through the convention area and into the banquet hall. She showed Dad and the others to the front row, then took me and Mom up a lift behind the stage.

"The awards aren't given until the end. When it's time, I'll go on first and introduce you, then you two can come out. Are you nervous?"

Tongue out.

"I'll tell you a secret. A sign-language interpreter will be on stage translating the program. Watch her instead of thinking about your speech."

By the time the assembly started, nearly every seat was filled. When my nerves cranked up, I watched the interpreter turn spoken words into hand gestures. She reminded me of Rumpelstiltskin, weaving straw into gold.

Finally, it was our turn. I don't remember Celeste's speech word for word, but it was basically what Hannah said at our tea party, about how she had seen me work through so many obstacles.

As Mom rolled me onstage, I scanned the crowd for familiar faces, but the bright lights made it hard to see anything. I finally was able to make out the front row. *My family*. They were all sitting up straight on the edges of their seats, watching me. Even Tucker was right side up. Dad smiled big and Hannah gave me a little wave.

Celeste presented me with a trophy, then took it back so Mom could hold Haha. Thankfully, the device found my eyes in like two seconds. My words filled the banquet hall:

When Celeste told me I was getting this award I was surprised, and I wondered why. I knew it wasn't because I'm good at assistive technology. I'm not.

I also knew it wasn't because I like assistive technology. I don't. I think the reason they gave me this is because of what assistive technology means to me.

Assistive Technology means people care about me.

My trips to the Center are like this: Celeste says she has another device to try. She pushes me up to a table, and I can't make it work. I cry. She says it's okay and makes me laugh. Then she tells me she'll go back and find something else. We both know we've been working on this forever, but she always comes back. And when she does, I know she cares.

At home, my family and friends try to make using my device into a game so I can forget how much work it is, and I know they care.

When Mom or Hannah holds me so I can spell, and it takes forever but they still do it, I know they care.

Every piece of assistive technology tells me someone thought about me and people like me and that they cared. They know my life and my voice matters.

Someday, I'll do things the regular way and won't need assistive technology, but until then, it's nice to know that there are people who care, because it makes all the difference.

Thank you.

It was awesome to have Haha read my speech because it meant I got to experience it with the audience. I saw the smiles and nods and knew today, my tiny, plain house was just right. I wanted to do this again, to watch people react to what Lexi Haas, author, had to say.

When it finished, I activated Kasey's sound file, and the voice of Donkey from *Shrek* filled the auditorium:

"I just know before this is over, I'm gonna need a whole lot of serious therapy."

The crowd laughed and clapped as Mom wheeled me across the stage. On the way off, I goosed the translator.

Celeste was now standing at the curtain with my trophy. She lifted an eyebrow but then smiled. We stared at each other for a second, and in that moment, I knew I had discovered my fourth gift.

Persistence. My fourth gift is persistence.

The fourth of my five gifts. I was nearly there.

There was no time to let that sink in. Instead, I soaked up the applause. There would be months, probably years, before the cheering was for me again. It was okay, though, because I knew if cheers were what I wanted, I had the determination, the stubbornness, the *persistence* to figure out how to get them.

When we reached the side of the stage, Mom turned my wheelchair so I could have a good view of my audience.

I scanned the crowd, side to side, up and down, until . . . *There*, by the back wall. The rest of the audience had settled, but a woman and two girls—one tiny and blonde, the other tall and dark-haired—stood clapping and cheering. I squealed.

When the ceremony was over, my family was waiting in the lobby. Everyone ran over to hug me.

"Great job, Lexi!" Hannah said.

The others chimed in with, "Yeah, great job!" and, "Awesome speech!" and I knew they meant it.

Then, out of nowhere, Anna and Elle were practically on top of me, jumping up and down.

"Lexi that was amazing!"

"Ouch! You're on my foot! I wanna say hi too. Move over or I'm telling!"

I laughed hard and threw my arms out. I had missed them so much.

"How in the world did you find out about this?" Mom asked.

"We got an invitation in the mail," Ms. Trejo said. "Didn't you send that?"

"It was from Lexi," Kasey said. "She wrote it!"

Everyone looked at me. I smiled.

Ms. Trejo cleared her throat. "Anna, Elle, do you want to tell Lexi why you haven't seen her this summer?"

"It was *her* fault," Elle said. "Anna told. I told her not to but—"

"I didn't mean to," Anna said. "It slipped out."

Mom looked confused.

Ms. Trejo shook her head. "So, it turns out that the girls were listening to *Harry Potter* books in Lexi's room."

"Oh! So that's what you three were up to. Those are Lexi's favorites," Mom said.

Mrs. Trejo leaned in. "They weren't supposed to. Dean and I had told them they weren't allowed to read them yet."

Mom bit her lip.

I looked away, too ashamed to meet Ms. Trejo's eyes. This rule was obviously important to them. To their family and to the way they operated as a unit. And I had ignored it. I had bypassed it without a second thought. For weeks, I had been so angry because my friends had not bothered to understand me. I felt like such a hypocrite.

"We weren't *reading*; we were *listening*," Elle interrupted. "And it woulda been fine if Anna had kept her big mouth shut."

Anna looked at her feet.

"They're great stories," Ms. Trejo continued. "And the first ones are fine, but we're just a little concerned about how dark the later books get. We wanted them to be a little older."

Mom put a hand on Ms. Trejo's shoulder. "I'm so sorry."

"Their punishment was that they weren't allowed to get together with Lexi for a month," Ms. Trejo continued. "I should have called you to talk about it, but you know how life gets."

Mom nodded and smiled.

Despite my lingering shame, I squealed and threw out my arms. Nothing in the world felt better than this. Not hearing my speech. Not soaking in the applause. Not even discovering my fourth gift. *Nothing* felt as good as knowing that all this time, my friends had wanted to be with me.

Ms. Trejo shrugged. "I thought about calling you to come have dinner with the group after Bible study some time, but I know that's not really your thing. Anyway, a month turned into two, and the next thing I knew we got Lexi's invitation in the mail. There was no way we could miss this!"

We stayed in the lobby, laughing and chatting. It didn't matter one nickel that I couldn't talk. I couldn't have gotten a word in between those two.

Finally, Tucker grabbed my trophy, held it to his chest, and said, "I'd like to thank the Academy!"

Kasey play-wrestled it from him and told him if he wanted his own trophy, he had to earn it.

Dad sighed. "We should probably leave before we're asked to leave."

Anna and Elle hugged me. Ms. Trejo and Mom made plans for us to get together—after I had served my sentence for what Dad called, "aiding and abetting a crime."

That night, I lay in bed thinking about the day. It had definitely been another *bam!* day. A great one. I now knew my fourth gift! Sure, my deadline was closing in, but there was still time. And, best of all, Anna and Elle were back! I squeezed my imaginary rock and the familiar rough edges pressed into my palm. Everything was gonna be okay.

On the other side of my wall, Dad's guitar was strumming "Summertime." I sang along in my head.

"I finally made the call to Richmond this afternoon," Mom said, cutting in. She took a deep breath, so deep I could hear it through the wall. "But not because of what was stolen. I made it because of what was left."

The last chord uncurled and hung in the air, fresh and sweet like a new leaf.

When it had finally settled, Dad said, softly, "I guess we had the same thought watching her today. There's so much going on in her head, but the challenges she'll face to be heard and understood . . ."

His voice drifted off for a minute then returned, stronger. "We owe her this. It's time to see if we can do devious."

Their voices faded. My head spun with the words. *It's time to see if we can do devious.*

That was it. My deadline was here. Maybe I didn't have all my gifts yet, but there was one thing I knew for sure. I was the sort of girl who made things happen. I was Lexi Haas, author.

There would be no more waiting for wind to catch my sails. It was time to take out the oars and row. I had to use my words to uncover their devious scheme.

I spent a restless night planning how to confront Mom.

CHAPTER 40
Age 13, 7 hours until surgery

After all the excitement of the evening, we're finally settled in our room. Gus ate his dinner in twelve seconds flat—we timed it—and is now stretched out on my bed with his legs in the air.

Dad says, "You look a little tense, Gus. Can I get anything to help you relax?"

Gus lolls his head to the side. He smiles and thumps his tail like he wants to say, "Sure! A soda would be awesome. Extra ice and a straw, please."

I've already written to Anna and Elle, and FaceTimed with Kali, Kasey, and Hannah. Now, Dad is calling Tucker.

He holds his phone so I can see.

"Whadup?" Tucker says. He leans in so I get a super close up of his nose, and I laugh.

"We're getting ready for bed," Dad says. "Tomorrow will be a long day."

"Are you ready, Lex?"

Tongue out.

"No words tonight?"

Tongue out.

"It's been a long day," Mom says. She tells him about the fire alarm, the MRI, and dancing with Steve.

"We've also been fielding messages from concerned Facebook friends all day," Dad adds.

"What kinds of messages?"

Dad pulls out his phone and reads them out loud.

Tucker smiles. "Whadaya think, Lex? Did the messages help?"

"Help? How could messages about infections and pain help someone who's about to have surgery?" Mom asks.

Tucker shrugs. "This is Lexi. She's gotta—you know—think through stuff. Even if it's hard stuff."

For a long second, Tucker and I lock eyes.

"Oh!" Mom says, as if she is just remembering to add some other *minor* detail. "She also got to message with the Trejo girls. It was good to hear from real friends."

Yes, *real* friends. The best.

"That's cool. Well, good luck tomorrow, kiddo. I'll be there in ten days so get ready. You didn't see *Captain America*, did you?"

I try to not smile. Tucker points a finger.

"You did!"

Guilty.

"You promised to wait! Well, you're just gonna have to sit through it again."

We say goodnight. Mom lifts me into bed. I close my eyes, and Dad reads me more good luck messages, but I'm thinking about what Tucker said. *Did the messages help?*

I didn't want to admit it but yeah, they kinda had. They reminded me of the crazy amount of preparation we've done. Last surgery, we fumbled through blindly. I was first—the very first—and that meant there was no one who could tell us what to expect. This time, we're ready.

If someone had straight-up told me the things those messages made me think about, I would have been ticked. In case you haven't noticed, I'm not great at taking advice. I don't want other people to tell me about my gifts, or to decide if I should have an operation that can at best can offer "possibly."

Of course, I'd never tell Tucker or he'd get a big head, but I'm glad he understands this about me. Maybe my Facebook friends understand too.

Right now, I have to put everything out of my head. It suddenly feels like morning is stalking me.

Deep breath in. My story. Breath out.

CHAPTER 41
Age 6, The Year of the Buttered Cat

The next morning, I tried to tell Mom I wanted to write, but she was distracted on her computer for hours. I simmered and waited. Kali fed me breakfast and lunch. I wondered if Mom was avoiding me or if she was researching more of her devious plan.

Late afternoon, Mom finally asked me what I'd like to do. I pointed to my cookie sheet.

Mom sighed. "I don't know, Lexi, I've been sitting all day. Wouldn't you like to go for a walk?"

I arched and squealed.

"Okay, okay, no walk."

I pointed again.

"Do you have something you need to say?"

Tongue out.

We sat together on my beanbag. The phone rang.

"Can anyone get that?"

No answer.

"I'll be right back."

She slipped out and ran to the kitchen, leaving me slumped sideways.

"Oh, hi, Anne! Thanks for calling back!"

She was off, chatting happily. "Right back" wasn't happening.

My long simmer finally came to a boil. I began to cry. Once started, the emotions rushed over me, and I was helpless to stop them. I howled like a wounded animal.

Mom flew into the den. "Lexi! Are you okay? Does something hurt?"

She searched my arms and legs. I continued to arch and screech.

Finally, she said, "Is this because you needed to tell me something?"

Tongue out. I sniffed.

"I'm sorry." She hugged me close until I quieted.

She pulled my cookie sheet to us. I pulled down letters as fast as I could.

Don't do devious! I know you're planning devious!

Mom was silent. I was sure she knew the gig was up, that I had overheard her plans. I looked at her, daring her to deny it, but she seemed genuinely confused.

I wrote, **I heard you and Dad talking about devious.**

Mom's eyes widened. I waited for the stammer of an apology, the fumbling of words as she tried to explain, but instead, there was a hint of a smile.

She hugged me. I struggled free.

"Lexi, I think you misunderstood, but I also think you deserve to know. What you heard was not *devious*. It was DBS. It's short for Deep Brain Stimulation, and it's a surgery Dad and I want to look into for you. In fact, we're scheduled for a consultation in Richmond next week."

I let that sink in for a long moment then wrote, **What is it?**

"DBS is a tiny implant they put into the brain to help cells fire normally. In your case, we're hoping it might give you better control of your muscles so you can do more things on your own."

Questions swirled in my head. *Will DBS help me walk? Talk? And when my body comes in, what then? Do they take the DBS out?*

But when I reached forward, what I asked was, **What things?**

Mom sighed. "That's the part we don't know. I've been watching and researching DBS for a couple of years now. There's still so much we don't know about how it works or even what it can potentially do."

Then, as if she read my mind, she said, "Lexi, we don't know if it can help you walk and talk. It's way too early to even guess about those things. First, we have to find out if the doc-tors will agree to give it a try."

We sat on the floor for several minutes, still and quiet.

Finally, Mom said, "I was going to talk to you about it be-fore the appointment."

I believed her.

"Right now, we aren't committed to anything more than finding out about it. Are you up for that?"

I stuck out my tongue slowly, and Mom hugged me.

CHAPTER 42
Age 6, The Year of the Buttered Cat

The week before my doctor's appointment in Richmond, Kali and Kasey started back to school. It was time for homeschool to get started, but Mom was too distracted to even take us shopping for supplies. There was a lot of planning, but for the first time I didn't have to hear it through the wall. Mom and Dad and I talked about it together. We decided Mom and I would make the five-hour drive by ourselves and that we would stay in a hotel the night after my appointment.

The morning of the trip, Mom woke me before sunrise. Dad followed us to the car, lugging a suitcase and a cooler of snacks and sandwiches. He kissed us and made Mom promise to text or call when we got there. He stood barefoot in the driveway with Luke and The Cat and waved as we pulled away.

The drive felt a little like my life history in rewind. We passed through Chapel Hill and then up I-95 into my birth state of Virginia. As we rolled across the border, I remembered a TV show Kali and I watched once about animals that migrate back to where they were born. Sea turtles, Canada geese, Atlantic puffins, and me.

I laughed out loud. Mom adjusted her rearview mirror so she could see me. I could see her smiling eyes in the mirror.

"Not much longer."

The scenery changed from pine trees to suburbs to city. Mom pointed to a tall building with *VCU* in yellow letters just off the highway.

"That's it!" she said, and I squealed.

Mom pulled up to the valet in front of the hospital. I had this weird feeling that I had been there before. It wasn't exactly a flashback. It was that prickly jumble of new and familiar.

Inside, the receptionist gave Mom a clipboard with papers to fill out and told us to have a seat.

Soon after, a dad came in with a boy who looked about Tucker's age. As the dad hunched over his clipboard, the boy rocked and flapped his hands. The dad reached into a bag, pulled out a carved wooden wand and handed it to his son. The boy stopped rocking, stopped shaking, and rubbed his hand over the wood.

I admired his swish-and-flick technique. He caught me watching and wordlessly cast a spell in my direction.

Oh, it is on.

I was pretty good with nonverbal spells myself. Not only that, I had perfected wandless magic.

I uncurled my finger. *Expelliarmus.*

Missed. I guess my aim still needed work.

The boy cast three in a row. I ducked, and they all sailed past.

I pointed again. *Tarantallegra.* The Dancing Feet Spell. If that worked, the boy would be tap dancing into his appointment. I laughed at that picture.

He jumped up. For a second, I thought my spell had hit its mark, but instead of dancing the boy lunged forward. He waved his wand at me. The spell flew over my head and hit the door to the back clinic. Right then, the door opened.

I squealed. *Nice use of the Alohomora Charm.*

The boy beamed.

"Lexi Haas," a nurse called.

Mom rolled me towards the door. I tried to wave goodbye but instead my arm flew out, blocking the doorway. Mom folded my arms to my chest and rolled me through.

Inside, the nurse led us to a tiny room where she took my pulse and blood pressure.

"The doctor will be in shortly," she said, closing the door behind her.

"Oh, I forgot to let Dad know we made it," Mom said. She pulled out her phone.

She was busy texting when I heard muffled voices outside the room. The door swung open. In swept a smiling man with a graying beard, bright, happy eyes, and a slightly crooked tie— the man from Mom's computer. The man from my dream.

CHAPTER 43
Age 13, 1 hour until surgery

It's 5 a.m.—an insane hour, by the way—but I'm dressed and in my chair. While Mom and Dad get ready, I look out the window at night sky and pouring rain. Occasionally, there's a crack of thunder and a flash reveals the houses across the street.

"I hope this lets up soon," Dad says, "or I don't know how we'll get to the hospital."

Downstairs, we stand at the front door and stare into the angry morning. Mom is at the front desk, and when she returns, she's frowning.

"There's no handicap accessible shuttle, so we'll have to make a run for it."

Dad throws up his hands. "How can a hospital not have an accessible shuttle?"

He rests his hands and forehead on the glass doors and stares into the parking lot. I'm certain he's thinking about grabbing me and making his own run for it—chucking me over his shoulder and Ubering to the airport. Hijacking a plane. Back to North Carolina. Back where the sun is already up, bright and hot. No rain, no storm. Just plain old, familiar North Carolina.

For a hot second, I hope he'll act on his fear. *Take me home. I was wrong. I'm not ready to make this kind of decision!*

I take a deep breath and think of my story. My evidence. My voice.

I smack his leg. When he looks at me, I point and smile. "Go!"

"Lexi, it's storming."

Ggguuhhh! "Go!"

Dad sighs.

Mom covers me with a plastic trash bag, hands Dad an umbrella, and smiles. "Race ya."

We dash into the rain with Gus loping beside us and Dad hot on our heels. My wheels whirl through puddles as we cross the street, dash pass the playground, slog up the long hill, then roll through the hospital entrance.

Finally.

Deep breath in. My story. Breath out.

CHAPTER 44
Age 6, The Year of the Buttered Cat

It took a minute to recover from my shock. I had only ever had that one glimpse of this man, that one flash of his picture on a website, but I was sure this was the same guy. He bent down so his eyes met mine.

"Lexi! It's been a long time since I last saw you! You probably don't remember me, but I'm Steve Shapiro."

Last saw me? That prickly feeling had been right. I *had* been here before.

I tried to say hi and wanted to say much more. All that came were grunts and groans. Dr. Shapiro nodded like he understood. When I finished, he took my hand and rubbed it for a long minute. He stood up and gave Mom a hug.

"It's great to see you again, Steve," Mom said.

Steve? She knew this guy well enough to call him by his first name.

Dr. Shapiro smiled. It was so warm, I felt like I knew him too.

I renamed him. *Steve.*

"We have a lot of catching up to do," Steve said.

The appointment felt more like a visit with an old friend and, as those kinds of visits usually do, went on much longer than any of us had planned.

I got the usual neurology exam—a check of my reflexes with the rubber hammer and a look into my eyes with a flashlight—but there was also a lot of talking, and for the first time ever in a doctor's appointment, I paid attention.

I found out I had actually seen Steve three times, but those visits were all when I was a baby. He said he had been busy with research on top of his full clinic schedule and that he wished he had more time to see kids like me.

"What about treatments?" Mom asked. "I've been watching the journals and haven't seen anything new."

"And you won't. This is too rare to get much attention from industry. They want to put their money where the numbers are." He stopped and sighed. "Most advances have come from parents taking matters into their own hands."

"Exactly." Mom handed the dog-eared papers to Steve. "Let's talk about Deep Brain Stimulation."

He smiled and pushed the papers back. "Susan, you know that's never been done on any of these kids. We hope to do studies on rats first—"

"And how long will *that* take? Five years? Ten? In the meantime, her childhood is slipping away. You know as well as I do her best shot at neurological repair is before puberty."

Mom! Seriously?

"And what does Lexi think about the idea?"

"She doesn't know much about it yet, but she's willing to at least find out. So, we should be too."

Steve looked at me and smiled. "You're interested in finding out about DBS?"

Tongue out.

"Tell me this, Lexi. How much do you know about your brain injury?"

Brain injury?

I had never heard those words together before. Separately, they were harmless. Together they were Mentos in Diet Coke. The jolt shot from the base of my spine.

My brain injury?

Steve looked at Mom. "Does she even know what happened?"

Mom's eyes met his then she looked away.

"Susan, she needs to know. Especially if you're considering something like DBS, but also because it's an important part of her life that she needs to understand."

"But she's six!"

"A very smart six," Steve said, smiling at me.

Mom nodded slowly.

"I'll tell you what. I'll talk with our neurosurgeon and see if she'll agree to bring Lexi back for more testing. If she thinks DBS might help, we can go from there, but insurance won't pay for it until Lexi turns seven, so we have time to gather opinions."

Mom folded the papers and nodded.

"In the meantime," he said, turning to me, "ask your Mom about jaundice. She has some things she needs to tell you so you completely understand."

Jaundice. Brain injury. DBS. The words swam together in my head.

Outside, Mom and I waited quietly for the valet to bring the van around. We drove to the hotel in silence. Not angry silence. Thinking silence.

This is it. The last car ride before I know. The last everything before I know. Do I want to know?

Mom rolled me into our room, flipped on the lights, and heaved our suitcase and cooler onto the bed. She bent over my chair and kissed me.

The last kiss.

"It's been a really long day. What can I do for you? Are you hungry or thirsty?"

Ggguuhhh. No more lasts! I have to know!

I stared at the suitcase.

Mom unzipped it, reached in, and held up my pajamas.

Ggguuhhh.

My teddy bear.

Ggguuhhh.

Finally, she held up my cookie sheet. I stuck out my tongue and arched my back.

She sighed. "Can we wait until tomorrow? We're both really tired."

GGGUUHHH.

Mom stared into my eyes for a long second, then pulled me onto her lap.

I reached for the board and pulled down letters.

"Jaundice," she read. She took a deep breath. "Do you know what it means?"

Ggguuhhh.

I want to know . . . I think . . . Do I? I can't go back and unknow.

I didn't spell that. I couldn't give her an open door.

"There are actually two definitions. There's medical jaundice, like Steve was talking about, but jaundiced also means bitter and resentful. The first one has a lot to do with you, but the second one isn't you at all. Lexi Haas, you are an enigma."

I reached for my board and pulled down more letters.

What's that?

"An enigma? It's something we can't easily explain."

Like my crazy body?

Mom nodded. I wrote some more.

And Virginia Dare?

"That's a good one. A historical enigma."

And buttered cats?

She laughed.

My mom has never had the luxury of watching me play outside, picking dandelions, and running, arms outstretched, to see the wind carry the seeds. Or of watching me chase fireflies as evening creeps in, wrapped in the sweet smell of warm earth and summer jasmine, and knowing she *should* call me in, that it's getting much too late. But I imagine that this was how she felt, watching my twisted, writhing body as I chased words instead of fireflies.

Finally, I knew it was time to go inside and that Mom wouldn't call me in. I reached forward and rapped my fist next to the first word I had written.

Jaundice.

I pulled down more letters.

Tell me.

Mom breathed in, as if savoring the last breath of warm, earthy air. "Okay. I think it's time you heard the whole story."

CHAPTER 45
Age 6, The Year of the Buttered Cat

Mom pushed aside my cookie sheet and gathered me in her lap like she did when I was little. She studied my eyes like a mother meeting her new baby for the first time. I knew she was thinking back to that April day when I was born.

"It was clear right from the beginning you were coming here with your own agenda. Dad was working out of town on weekdays. He was on his way home when I went into labor three weeks early. Once you decided it was time to be born, there was no stopping you.

"You made your appearance twenty-one minutes after we got to the hospital—barely long enough to get into a birthing room. Your first moments weren't pretty, though. Your breathing was fast and light. The nurses whisked you off to the newborn nursery for oxygen.

"My arms ached from the emptiness. I wanted to hold you so badly, but instead of cuddling you in our room, Dad and I stood by the nursery window and waved at you, kicking and screaming under an oxygen tent. You had a huge, swollen bruise on your forehead, a souvenir from your fast exit. When Dad called home to tell the kids you were here, he joked that their new sister looked like an angry drunk in a bar brawl."

I laughed hard, and my arms and legs went wild.

Mom waited for me to calm, then continued. "By nighttime, you were still in the newborn nursery. Dad went home to be with the other kids. I was getting ready for bed when a nurse came in to say you were a little jaundiced—or yellow—probably because of the bruise and that they would put you under some special lights to help clear it up.

"The next morning, Dad brought the kids to meet you. By then you were breathing fine and had given up the fight for a long, deep sleep—so deep you didn't even wake up to nurse.

"The doctor phoned in to tell the nurses to discharge you. He told us to bring you to his office in three days for a checkup. That's when Tucker wheeled you NASCAR-style toward the exit until a nurse revoked his license

"Over the next three days, I don't think your head ever hit your crib because your siblings were all fighting over who would hold you. Dad had to go back to work in Chapel Hill. He didn't want to leave, but I told him that you were so easy, we would be fine. By Monday, I could barely wake you to nurse, and your skin had turned a deep yellow-bronze.

"That afternoon, I took you in for your checkup. By then I was worried. I told your doctor, 'She sleeps around the clock! And look at her skin, she looks like she's been on a beach vacation!'

"He laughed and told me I was just an overanxious mom. He said I didn't need to worry about the jaundice, that it would eventually go away.

"And he was right, the jaundice did clear up, but it took nearly three weeks." She stopped for a minute and sighed. "Are you sure you want to hear all this tonight? We can finish tomorrow."

Ggguuhhh.

I was exhausted, but I had never been more awake than I was at that moment.

Mom swallowed hard and continued. "Well, your early struggles seemed behind us, and we settled into the chaos of a family of seven. But after a few months, we noticed you weren't reaching out to touch things or trying to roll over. Also, you went from sleeping *all* of the time to sleeping *none* of the time. Dad and I had to tag team sleep just to get a couple of hours of rest each night.

"Your doctor finally agreed that something didn't seem right. He sent you to a neurologist, but she didn't know what was going on, either. At that point, I took matters into my own hands. I got a copy of your medical records and dragged you and your brother and sisters to every children's hospital within a day's drive.

"We saw all sorts of specialists who ordered dozens of tests, but no one could tell me what was going on. Our medical bills were adding up along with the stress. Work suffered, because we were so focused on finding out what was happening with our sweet baby. We lost our house and cars and moved to North Carolina, but I pressed on, searching for answers that I knew had to be there.

"At night, when you and I were the only ones still awake, I pored over your medical records and searched the internet, hoping to find anything that made sense, anything that could pull it all together.

"One night, I was staring at the doctor's notes from your first days, and something struck me. All his notes were typed, except for the ones from that first appointment. For the first time, I wondered if your records had been changed. I tried to reconstruct that visit, moment by moment in my head. What did we talk about? What did he want to cover up?

"Finally, it came to me. Jaundice. You had been really jaundiced, but there was nothing about it in his notes. There was nothing about it in the hospital records. I went back to my computer and searched some more, until one night I found

Steve's website. Suddenly, it all made sense. You had been poisoned."

I nearly arched out of Mom's arms.

Poisoned? Who would poison a baby? Did you call the police? Were they arrested?

Now I understood why Mom had leaned over the porch railing and vomited that night. My stomach lurched.

Mom put a hand on my chest and waited for my body to relax. "Let me explain. Lots of new babies have jaundice. It's caused by bilirubin, which is made by your body. Most of the time it's harmless. But if the doctor isn't careful . . ." Her voice turned squeaky, and she trailed off.

Don't stop! I flailed, hitting her in the ribs.

She squeezed me and cleared her throat. "If the doctor isn't careful and lets the bilirubin get too high or lets it go on for too long, it can get into the baby's brain and poison certain areas. Once these areas are damaged, they can't be fixed. The baby is left with a condition called kernicterus."

She went on to say that people with kernicterus can have cerebral palsy or deafness or both and that while my hearing was spared, a part of my brain that controls movement was not.

I heard this part, but I was stuck on what she said before that. *Once these areas are damaged, they can't be fixed.*

Those words settled over me. I knew they wanted to seep into me, to become a part of me. I had to keep them out.

I stared into Mom's eyes, pleading with her.

No! That's not true! My body is coming! I'll catch up! I just need to find one more gift, and it will be here! It's coming! Right? It's coming!

I needed to hear the words. She *had* to say the words. *Don't worry. You'll catch up.* She didn't know I had been searching for gifts for a year, or for my body for a lifetime. But it didn't matter because I could see the answer right there in her eyes.

I couldn't keep the words out any longer. *Once these areas are damaged, they can't be fixed.*

And just like that, Lexi Haas, the person I thought I knew, began to dissolve. Bits and pieces pixelated then vanished into nothingness. Fingers and hands, then toes and feet.

This was not how this was supposed to end. I needed a different ending! *Please, let there be a different ending!*

They say people who are about to die see their lives flash before their eyes. But in that moment, what I saw was the life I was supposed to have. Little slices of ordinary that should have been mine.

I was riding a sparkly blue bicycle, knees scratched, and my face twisted with concentration. Dad was jogging hunched over beside me as he held my seat. He whispered, "You can do it! You're doing it!" He faded behind me as I peddled off on my own. Strands of sweaty hair whipped across my face.

Then I saw myself a little older, sitting—or half sitting—in Ms. Joann's class. I was nearly leaping from my seat, my hand punching the air as I cried out, *"Choisissez-moi! Choisissez-moi!"* until Ms. Joann chose me to answer her question.

Then, I was maybe twelve or thirteen, at the mall with Anna and Elle. I was holding an ice cream cone, trying to lick the sticky, strawberry stream dribbling onto my hand, but I was laughing so hard, and they were laughing so hard, I couldn't keep up.

And finally, worst of all, that same version of me was gathered with my family at the dinner table. I couldn't make out the conversation because everyone was talking at once. I must have asked Kasey to pass the potatoes because she did. And Tucker probably said something aggravating because I punched him in the arm. He laughed and punched me back.

I watched us all for a few moments. Each of us eating, talking, laughing. In this world, I wasn't at the center. I wasn't the planet that couldn't exist without its six moons orbiting closely. This was seven individual units going about life together, but also independently.

This was not the life I was going to have. This was the life that was stolen.

My arms and legs were just tiny particles now, my chest and head were fading. There was nothing left to hold them together. The person, the entity, that had been me was nearly gone.

This is NOT how this is supposed to be. This is NOT how this is supposed to end.

Mom pulled me onto her shoulder and wrapped her arms around me. I buried my face in her shirt, and we let our tears come. My body was shaking, heaving as I sobbed.

Mom held onto me for dear life. Her tears fell onto my shoulder. They tickled a little, and I found myself concentrating on each tear as it made its way from my shoulder and down my back before finally rolling off and pooling at the back of my knee. Drop after drop of pure, distilled love. The price for caring so much.

Slowly—so slowly that at first I didn't notice—I began to reform. Bits and pieces that made up my shoulders and chest and arms and legs reappeared. The pieces merged together and became solid.

You can do this. You. Can.

I opened my eyes and found I could still see. I took a deep breath and found I could still breathe. The pain was still there, deep and throbbing like the phantom ache of a missing limb. Or a missing life.

I slid from Mom's shoulder and onto her lap. I was whole again. And nothing, not one thing, was different.

I was the same kid I had been before I knew the truth. I was the same kid who couldn't walk or talk or control her body, but I was also the kid gifted with memory. And words. And humor. And persistence.

And *optimism*. The new gift jumped in line all on its own. My Aha! moment. I smiled.

CHAPTER 46
Age 13, 45 minutes until surgery

In the hospital lobby, Mom peels the trash bag off me, and underneath I'm mostly dry.

Mom is soaked. She runs a hand across her face. "I was wondering if I'd get my jog in today."

Gus shakes his head and the shudder runs down his back and to his tail, like a wave. He is smiling.

Dad is not.

Mom pries the umbrella from Dad's hand and kisses his cheek. "You worry too much."

Steve is waiting for us in pre-op. He's wearing scrubs and his game face. I want someone to crack a joke. *Please, Dad, tell a joke!*

"We decided to swim over this morning," Mom says, squeezing rain from her ponytail.

We all laugh.

Mom helps me change into another ridiculous butt-baring gown, and the day suddenly gets real. My sinkhole of fear is trying to grow, but I focus on my rock, and it holds steady.

Today, the IV goes in easily. There are more forms to sign and a parade of nurses, techs, and *-ists*.

There have been plenty of phone pings to keep Dad busy. First, there were texts from my siblings wishing me good luck. Next, texts from Anna, Elle, and Ms. Trejo. I have already repeated those in my head like fifty times.

Right now, Dad is flooded with message pings—notes from all over the world, sending love, hope, prayers, and good vibes. I want to hear them all. I think I understand a little better about the prayers offered up from strangers now, about the need to *do* something.

Of course, Dad is responding to every single message. Thirteen years ago, in the craziness of my birth and the days after, he felt like a helpless bystander. It doesn't matter one nickel that what happened to me wasn't his fault. Maybe his obsessive need to do something is *his* price for caring so much.

Finally, the techs stand by my gurney ready to roll me to the operating room, and my stomach lurches. I remind myself of all the planning, all the research.

You've done this before, and you were only seven.

We're moving now.

But I didn't know what was ahead of me. It was all just a big circus then.

The first surgery, all my family was there. The media was there too, snapping pictures as I rolled off. It was like starring in a TV show, and at some point, someone offstage was gonna say, "Cut."

I laugh out loud at that, and Mom and Dad look at me with their heads tilted. I study their faces. *Please, please don't let me forget their faces!*

My caravan begins to speed up, and suddenly everything is happening too fast.

White coats swish by. *Hurry. Hurry.*

The wheels on my gurney whirl over linoleum tiles. *Hurry, Hurry. Finish your story. Before you go in. Before it's too late.*

CHAPTER 47
Age 6, The Year of the Buttered Cat

After Mom finished telling my birth story, I sat motionless on her lap for a long time. She didn't talk or try to move me. We just sat. I let my story seep in. That story that had been hidden, kept separate for so long, needed to become part of who I was. The fragmented tale of NASCAR Tucker had been my whole birth story for so long. Now I could see why it had been plucked out of all that sadness to be the one carefree reminder of that day.

But there was still one thing that didn't make sense. There was one more thing I needed to know. I lunged towards my cookie sheet.

Mom jumped, like I had startled her from her thoughts. "What? What's wrong?"

I uncurled my finger. She pulled the cookie sheet onto my lap and held my wrist.

I pulled down a few letters, but now I was dragging bricks. After two words, I stopped.

My doctor

Mom gave me a little squeeze. "Lexi, I've spent your entire life trying to forget about him. Let's not go there."

Ggguuhhh. I reached forward.

ALL Even Lou.

She looked at me with wide eyes, then sighed. "Okay. You're right. You need to hear your whole story."

She pushed aside my cookie sheet. In her face, I saw sparks from a smoldering fire that had been prodded back to life.

"The part about your brain injury is the only part we know for sure. But there's also the mystery of your missing medical records, and we can only guess about what happened there.

"As for the hospital, I don't think there was anything intentional. That day, I think they were overwhelmed, got sloppy, and took shortcuts. The nurse who said she would put you under the lights probably got busy and forgot. I don't think anyone ever wrote about jaundice in your hospital records. But the doctor . . . the doctor was a different story."

She held her breath like she was trying to control the flames licking inside.

"I think at one point there *was* mention of jaundice in his notes, because your entire first visit was about how yellow you were! When I started asking for medical records, he probably panicked. He knew he hadn't monitored your jaundice. He also knew that if I ever figured it out, he'd be in big trouble. So, he got rid of the only evidence he had—the records from your first visit.

"And it worked out for him, didn't it?" She laughed a little, but it was a cold laugh. "It threw us off the trail for a couple of years. Once I figured it out, there was no evidence that he had ever seen you jaundiced, so he couldn't be held responsible. For years, we tried to find a way to hold him accountable. We went to one attorney after another. But in the legal system, missing evidence is basically no evidence."

No evidence? Didn't she see the absurdity, the *obvious* flaw in that? I flailed. How could destroying my records wipe out my very existence? *What about* me? *I'm still here!* I twisted and groaned. *Please look at me! I AM the evidence!*

My life flashed before me again, but this time it was real life.

I was propped up on pillows on my parents' bed. Dad picked up my hand and strummed it over his guitar so I could feel how a hand *should* move. Then, I was strapped in my sparkly blue wheelchair, and Tucker was running with me up and down our driveway so I could feel the wind in my face. Finally, I was curled on Mom's lap, and with a shaky hand, I drug plastic letters around a cookie sheet so that I could have a voice.

Could one stroke of a pen, one person's desperate attempt to bury the truth, erase a lifetime?

I flailed harder, but the fire had consumed her.

"There are deadlines for how long families have to file this sort of lawsuit. After trying four times to take this to court, I just wanted to move on and focus on treatments. Lou Lattimore was Dad's last shot at bringing your doctor to justice. The legal system failed us, but if your doctor has a conscience at all, he's living with guilt. He knows he caused your brain injury and that he covered it up. Dad says there's a cold, dark place in hell for people like that."

She started to cry again. She buried her face in my hair and rocked me hard and fast as she sobbed. We were transported in time, together, to that moment on our front porch when she first discovered what happened.

I wanted to make this better for her, to tell her that everything was gonna be okay. *I* would be okay. Even without my body, I would have an amazing life. I was one-hundred percent sure. After all, I was a gifted optimist.

Of course, I couldn't tell her I knew all five of my gifts and how awesome that felt, after over a year of searching to finally know! She hadn't given up until she knew, and neither had I. Knowing my gifts wouldn't bring me my body but finding them still felt important.

I tried to pat Mom's back, but instead wound up punching her in the ribs. She continued to sob.

After a few minutes, I knew there was only one way to get her attention. I drank in deep breaths of air and let fly an impressively loud burp.

She sat up, laughing even as the tears continued. Finally, she wiped away the last few and smiled. "We should've told you before. After we saw Steve, Dad and I rarely spoke of it again, and only with each other. It was as if saying it out loud would somehow set it in cement. Early on, there was hope that you might outgrow some of it, that your young brain would find a way to rewire. So we chose to focus on that instead.

"By the time you were three, I knew we had to tell you, but I didn't want to kill your spirit. From the very beginning you were the hardest worker I had ever known. You just pushed ahead no matter what obstacles were put in front of you. I should have had more faith in you, given you more credit. I should have known you persevered *despite* not knowing, not *because* you didn't know. Does that all make sense?"

I stuck out my tongue and smiled.

Mom looked at her watch and gasped. "It's nearly eleven and you haven't had dinner yet. What kind of mother am I?" She reached for the cooler.

Ggguuhhh.

"No? Aren't you hungry?"

Ggguuhhh.

She looked into my eyes for a long moment then shifted so that she was lying down with me curled in her arms. I guess we fell asleep like that, because I don't remember anything else of that night.

CHAPTER 48
Age 13, 5 minutes until surgery

My gurney has stopped outside a set of wide double doors. On the wall, a sign reads, *RESTRICTED ACCESS—STAFF ONLY.* Red letters. All caps. I think they mean it.

Mom and Dad lean over. I see fear in their eyes.

I think back to our flight to Missouri—could it really have been only three days ago?—and to Bob from the parks department.

"Sinkholes don't happen just anywhere. They happen in places where the rock below the surface has eroded away, leaving a cavity that will eventually collapse in on itself."

Wait! Please, *please* stop!

I realize I've told my story wrong. My sinkhole didn't start when I found out about my stroke. It was way before that. My sinkhole started in that hotel room six years ago. It started when I finally learned the truth about my birth. That doctor eroded my foundation in ways that even *I* don't understand. But it has to stop. *Here. Today.* I can't be invisible any longer. I have to get my voice. I have to be the evidence.

"Are you ready?" Mom asks. Her voice is barely a whisper.

"Yeah!"

I belt it out, loud and strong. It echoes in the hall, and Gus barks.

Mom smiles at me, and I study her brown eyes. I don't remember when those lines first appeared in the corners. And her auburn hair is now tinged with gray. Is that new? I guess it's true that worry can age a person. I want to reach up and hug her. To stroke her hair and tell her everything is going to be fine. There are no guarantees in there, but we've done everything we can possibly do. We've buttered the whole cat.

Dad puts a hand on my forehead then slowly combs his fingers through my curls.

The double doors swing open, and I roll through.

Nearly there. Deep breath in. My story. Breath out.

CHAPTER 49
Age 6, The Year of the Buttered Cat

The morning after I learned my whole story, I woke up in that hotel bed, still in my clothes. The drapes were open, and sun streamed in. Mom was already up working at her laptop. When she saw my eyes open, she leaned over to kiss me. Her hair tickled my cheeks.

My stomach wasted no time reminding me that I had missed dinner. I glanced towards the cooler and opened my mouth wide.

"I bet you're starving!" She opened the cooler, poked around inside, and closed it.

Then Mom did something that she never did. She called room service.

We ordered scrambled eggs and waffles with real strawberries, not the frozen soggy ones. Mom got coffee, and I got chocolate milk. We sat together on the bed, and she fed me like she used to, all curled up on her lap.

In the early afternoon, we loaded up the van and drove

home, Mom singing to the radio and me, with a bad case of kernicterus, humming along in my head.

The pain from the news wasn't completely gone. The tears, the frustration, the anger would all rush back, sometimes at the most unexpected times. But there were years ahead to deal with all that. This new day was for celebrating accomplishments. Hannah had been right. They were the feathers in my cap *and* the birds I had met along the way. And those weren't small things.

When we finally got home, it was nearly dark. My whole family was standing in the driveway holding paper signs that said, *Welcome Home* and *We missed you.*

At first, I thought Tucker's sign was upside down, but when I looked closer I saw that Tucker was upside down, walking on his hands with his sign taped to his shirt.

He cartwheeled to the van, and for a hot second, I was back at the beach, watching him cartwheel down the sand. I thought about the promise I had made 13 months before. *When my body comes in, I'm gonna do that too.* I didn't know how, and I didn't know when, but I knew someday I would keep that promise.

Kali took me from my car seat and hugged me. Luke bounded towards us with The Cat in hot pursuit.

I watched The Cat figure-eighting Luke and thought of

prophecies and gifts and buttered cats. It would be years before I understood it all. I was pretty sure buttering the cat
was not about fixing a broken relationship. What I didn't yet
understand was that it also was not about fixing me. In fact,
it wasn't about me at all. Buttering the cat was a step towards
fixing Mom.

As the sun melted behind treetops, I sunk into Kali's
shoulder and thought, *Life could be a lot worse.*

And that wasn't even my optimism talking.

CHAPTER 50
Age 13, Recovery, Day 1

I wake to searing pain from my neck to my belly. It pulses. *Snakes!* I try to shake off the one slithering up my back. Writhing makes it bite harder, so I try to lie still.

I open my eyes a crack, but they're heavy. I can sort of make out a garland strung over my window. Is it Christmas? Where am I?

There's a fuzzy, flurry of movement in the room, and I realize I'm not alone.

A dog—or is it a wolf? Or a coyote?— jumps onto my bed and lies across my legs. How did *that* get in here? I flail, and the snake sinks in its fangs. The animal on my legs won't budge. He lies there like it's his *job* or something. An auburn-haired lady grabs my hand.

"Squeeze. Once for one hit of morphine, twice for two, three for the max."

Three squeezes.

She pushes a button once, twice, three times.

The pulsing pain continues. Consciousness is trickling back. *There are no snakes.*

I open my eyes wider, but the room is still blurry. The animal scooches up from my legs to lick my face.

"Not the face!" the woman says. She leans in to kiss me, and her hair tickles my cheeks.

"Well, it's about time," says a man's voice.

The animal licks me some more. My eyes focus and my first clear image is of a pink, slobbery tongue. A black dog is draped across my chest.

The smell hits my nose all at once. Memories of a black dog skidding between my dad's legs flood back.

"Oh geez. Someone crack a window please!" the man says.

Dad! And Gus! My farting, ADD service dog, Gus.

Dad leans over me. His T-shirt is pulled up over his nose, but his eyes are smiling. "Trying to wake you after sedation is leashing—"

The cat! It's leashing the cat!

My eyes dart from Mom to Dad. *My* Mom. *My* Dad.

I flail, and white-hot pain shoots up my side and into my neck. The morphine should kick in any second now. I remember that from last time. Last. Time. It's a blurry flurry of memories.

Hee hee! Blurry flurry. Flurry blurry. Flurrrrrr . . .

CHAPTER 51
Age 13, Recovery, Day 3

Three days in and the pain is much better. Not gone, but better. I'm sitting up in bed, and Mom is squeezing a juice box into the corner of my mouth. My memory is back, good as ever. Well, except for the ice fishing contest. I can only recall a few filmy images, like I'm underwater looking up to the surface. That's okay. I'm fine with not remembering that.

"Good morning, Lexi! You know what today is!"

I squeal. It's Brian and his nurse, Jill. They've come to turn on my new stimulator. I try to remind myself this is just act two in my three-act play.

Jill holds the programmer to my belly, and Brian pushes a few buttons.

DBS programming is complicated. I understand it best if I think of it as controlling a hurricane—a good hurricane. Brian can change things like how much land will be hit, how much rain will fall, and how long the water will stick around afterwards. Only the rain, *obviously*, is electrical stimulation.

"It's on," he announces. "Lexi, I'm only going to turn it up a little, in case steam comes out of your ears or something."

We all laugh but I wish there *would* be steam—something to *see*. As it is, it feels like nothing. *It all happens in the third act.* Yes, the mind-numbingly dull third act is where the ending will unfold. I think about my voice. My story. My evidence.

I'm suddenly aware of another person standing by my bed.

"Hi Lexi. I'm Jan, one of the physical therapists. We're going to try to get you up in a gait trainer and walk around a bit."

Gait trainer? Seriously? It's been three days!

I screech in protest, but despite my complaints, within a few minutes I'm strapped into this contraption that looks like a walker an old person might use, only with a bunch more straps and supports. It helps me stand up straight and tall.

I'm taking cautious steps down the hall. Gus is trotting beside me, barking his encouragement and sidling up to anyone who will pet him. Dad doesn't notice, because he's recording my every step on his phone. He's crying a little, and I guess I am too. Because I'm a lot like my dad.

Maybe it's all in my head, but I think my steps seem a little easier. That makes me laugh. *Of course, it's all in your head. Obviously.*

CHAPTER 52
Age 13, Recovery, Day 6

I can't believe it's been nearly a week since surgery. Dad posted that video of me walking in my gait trainer, and more than 4,000 people have watched it. They're probably thinking what I was thinking. *Walking three days after surgery? Seriously?*

Yesterday, Dad had to go back home to North Carolina. He took Gus so that Mom wouldn't have to take care of both of us. Also, Gus had to get back to his part-time job. And that reminds me, I haven't finished telling you about The Cat.

A few years ago, after a long, happy life, Luke passed on peacefully. He was indifferent to The Cat to the very end. When we brought Gus home two years later, The Cat greeted him at the door like he was welcoming an old friend. He figure-eighted his legs, and when Gus lay down, The Cat kneaded his belly.

Gus, as you probably guessed, does not *do* indifference. He swiped The Cat in with one paw and licked him top to bottom. Unbuttered. I guess Gus likes his cats plain.

Ever since, Gus has been moonlighting with The Cat. It gives him something to do when I'm asleep. I can only imagine how happy The Cat was when Dad walked in with Gus this week.

That's The Cat's happily ever after, but mine is just beginning. This place is beginning to get old, but most days Mom has been able to sneak me out. She rolls me up to the Liberty Memorial, and we watch Kansas City life—plain old ordinary Kansas City life—unfold below us. When we roll back in the hospital, Mom stops at the nurses' station to check for mail. Usually I have a pile of cards from Facebook friends, and Mom tapes them to my wall. It helps cheer my room up.

Brian and Jill have come by every day to program my stimulator. I still can't feel much, but here's the thing. Yesterday, when I raised my arm to feel my buzz cut, I touched my head. With my hand! For the first time ever, I rubbed my head. And today, I even held my head up for a few seconds all on my own. Mad skills, right?

So far, my voice is no different than before surgery. I can still huff out a few words, but they aren't any clearer or stronger. That might get better over time, but if I have control of my head and maybe even more than that, I should at least be able to use Haha. And that's where my voice, my story, my evidence really begins.

CHAPTER 53
Age 13, Recovery, Day 7

Mom is holding up her phone, slowly turning it all the way around my room. She stops and focuses in on the *We Love You, Lexi* garland over my window.

"You hung it up!" Elle and Anna both shout from the phone.

Mom turns the screen back to me. I stick out my tongue and sit up as tall as I can in my wheelchair.

This is the first time we've talked since surgery.

Before we FaceTimed them, Mom covered up my head with one of the rainbow bandannas they gave me. They admired my fashion statement and filled me in on everything I've missed in Charlotte. Which, they promised, is nothing.

Now, Mom is giving them a tour of my room. When she's done, we make plans to get together as soon as I get home.

Just as we're about to hang up, Elle asks to see my head.

I take a deep breath, I haven't even gotten up the courage to look at myself yet, much less share my new look outside of the hospital.

Elle clasps her hands and gives me a big, cheesy smile. "Pretty please."

I laugh then give Mom the thumbs up.

She carefully removes my bandanna. Elle squeals.

"Your hair looks amazing like that!"

"In a few weeks, you'll look just like Emma Watson when she had her hair short," Anna says.

I smile big, even though I knew for sure Emma Watson didn't have wires bulging in her neck or spots where hair would never grow back.

Suddenly, five or six -ists file into my room. It's the daily hospital rounds.

"Gotta go," Mom says, waving. "We'll see you guys in a few days."

The head -ist, is a short, freckled, red-haired man. Over the last few days, he's grown on me. I don't trust him yet, but I like him. He asks Mom questions and checks out my stitches.

Before they leave, he turns to Mom, "Someone said they saw you two off property again yesterday."

Mom nods. "We went to the Ronald McDonald House for brownies."

I love how she doesn't even try to hide our jailbreak.

He and the other -ists are shaking their heads even as she nods.

"You can't just leave hospital property like that—"

"It's a mental health break."

Truth. I need a) sun on my cheeks and b) fresh air in my lungs, not this super-scrubbed hospital air. Without those breaks, I'd go bananas.

"I could say we won't leave again, but we probably will."

Obviously.

I can tell the redheaded *-ist* is trying to look stern, but there's a little smile behind his and-I-mean-it glare. Finally, he sighs. "Well, at least get a pass when you go out so we can find you if we need to."

Mom nods. They leave. We fist bump.

I still have a problem with *-ists*. How do you build trust after a start like mine? How do you ever put down your guard, climb out of your sinkhole, and let people help?

It's tricky, but for me it's two parts. Both involve the future.

Part One is finding doctors who are willing to chase answers and push for solutions, even when those answers and solutions don't exist yet. It starts with finding doctors who will butter the whole cat.

In fact, I've started a list. Okay, I'll say it—an *-ist* list. *Doctors I Trust.* Since I started coming here to Kansas City, my *-ist* list has grown to a staggering five. My goal is double digits, but that's gonna take a while.

I mean, my *brain* knows that most doctors are caring and trustworthy and all those things that doctors should be. But my story is not just stuck in my brain. It's woven into every part of who I am. I don't think unweaving is possible. Or necessary. I just need to keep weaving new, better stories on top of the old one until that old story fades.

Then there's Part Two, and that is all about paying it forward to save the next baby. It's me, telling my story. After the first surgery and all the publicity, we found our way to other families with familiar stories. Innocent babies, sloppy doctors, unmonitored newborn jaundice, a lifetime of disability. Why hadn't we heard this before? Why wasn't it screamed from a balcony or at least a newspaper headline?

Turns out, it was the legal system. Most of the time, when this happens, there's a lawsuit. The cases are usually cut and dried and rarely make it to the courtroom. Settlements are reached. Damages are set and along with it, a gag order. A legally binding agreement that families must never, *ever* tell their story publicly.

The doctor silences the baby. The legal system silences the rest of the family.

So, it continues to happen. With no one left to tell the story, it continues to happen, the evidence swept away like inconvenient crumbs.

Until me. My doctor may have destroyed my medica records but there was one crucial piece of evidence left behind. *Me.* I am the evidence. Lexi Haas, author, is here to tell her story.

CHAPTER 54
Age 13, Recovery, Day 8

I'm sitting in my wheelchair in the hospital activity room. Three fat spotlights shine down on me with such intensity, I feel naked. There are also cameras and fuzzy microphones on poles and way too many people for this space.

This was all Steve Shapiro's idea. Yesterday, Mom and I came back from our daily jailbreak to find him admiring my collection of cards. He didn't even ask where we had been, even though I'm sure when he hugged us, we smelled of mulch, and catmint, and fresh air.

He inspected my stitches, then slumped into a chair and smiled. Steve has this certain smile when he has an idea. It's playful and mischievous, and his eyes light up like a kid planning a candy heist.

Mom recognized it too, because she said, "Okay, Steve. What are you up to?"

Steve picked up my room service menu. "Have you tried the chicken nuggets? I hear they're pretty good."

Mom pushed the menu away from his face. "Steve. What's up?"

He smiled again then took a deep breath. "I was thinking of getting a news crew out here to do a story about Lexi's surgery."

Mom didn't say anything, so Steve continued, "It would be good for the community to see what we're doing here at the hospital, and at the same time, create some awareness about kernicterus. You know . . . like last time." He turned to me. "This is only a small local station, but you never know."

I swallowed hard. I knew. Local news becomes national news, and before long I'd have even *more* people watching me. I looked at Mom.

She smiled and held up her hands. "I'm staying out of it. This is your call."

Part of me—a lot of me—wanted to put on another movie, order up some of those chicken nuggets, and call it a day. I wanted to be a regular kid. Was that too much to ask? But that voice in my head would not shut up. *Part Two is about paying it forward to save the next baby. It's me, telling my story.*

Deep breath in. My story. Breath out.

There's a long mirror in the activity room. One of the camera guys is covering it with a drop cloth, "To reduce glare," he explains.

Before he's done, I get my first glimpse of myself since surgery. The bright lights spare nothing. I have no idea what Elle found so amazing about *this*. My hair has grown in enough to look like a dark brown buzz cut. On top are two jagged incisions. My neck bulges with the wires. As predicted, I look like Frankenstein. It's one thing to frighten children on the street. Am I ready to share this with the whole world?

I don't have long to think about it before a producer positions Steve, Brian, Mom, and the reporter around me. Another light flashes on and the cameraman says, "In three, two, one . . ."

CHAPTER 55
Age 13, Recovery, Day 9

Mom, Steve, and I are hanging out in my room eating chicken nuggets. The local news is blaring from my TV. It's super boring, but our story is finally supposed to air tonight, and we don't want to miss it.

Just before the news is over, the anchor says, almost offhandedly, that they want to show us some cutting-edge procedures going on at the children's hospital. As he talks, a picture of me flashes on the screen. I wince. Mom squeezes my hand.

The interview is short. Too short. Personally, I don't think the reporter has done her job. She doesn't know anything about DBS and doesn't even mention kernicterus. She talks to Mom and Steve the most, and Brian explains how the DBS is supposed to help. It seems like I am mostly there for show.

The reporter doesn't ask me a single question until the very end. Finally, she turns to me and says, "Lexi, do you have optimism about your future now?"

I take a deep breath and watch myself squirm in my wheelchair. I admit, she caught me a little off guard. How do you answer that sort of ridiculous, loaded question?

I never do look at her. Instead, I turn to Steve and smile. I stick out my tongue. He smiles and sticks out his too.

They cut to a commercial. Mom turns off the TV.

"Well, that was . . . interesting," she finally says. Then she says what I am thinking. "Too bad they used your platform as a promo for the hospital."

Steve shrugged. "We just have to keep working away at it. Keep trying to get the message out." He washes his hands in my sink and pulls paper towels from the dispenser. "Anyway, I wasn't completely wrong. The chicken nuggets *are* good."

CHAPTER 56
Age 13, Recovery, Day 10

It's now been ten days since surgery and guess what? *I'm. Going. Home.* Today! Tonight, I will sleep in my own bed with Gus snoring loudly on the floor. And tomorrow, I'll get to see Anna and Elle in person.

In the past couple of days, I've traded pain for boredom. There's been too much time for stuff to stew in my head. One thing that I keep going back to is that reporter's stupid question. *"Do you have optimism about your future now?"*

I've thought a lot about that word. *Optimism.* I even had Mom google it.

op·ti·mism *n. hopefulness and confidence about the future or the successful outcome of something.*

Exactly what I expected, but still, my brain gets hung up, crazy enough, on that little *n.* up front. Noun. I know. I get it. Abstract noun, blah blah blah. I understand that. *Obviously.*

But this doesn't sync with *my* optimism. This googled version is a stupid, empty meme of hearts and rainbows and perky slogans like, "If you can dream it, you can achieve it!" or "Life is nothing but attitude."

I call bull and here's why.

In the last few months I've known despair that, even in my wheelchair, buckles my knees. Hopelessness so deep, it's like a stomach that's never been fed. A heart that's never been loved. And yeah, a voice that's never been heard. Still I know, *I know* I'm an optimist.

I don't think optimism is about dancing through life, never witnessing the sinkhole of my fears. Optimism is finding myself in the bottom of that hole and feeling around in the darkness until I find the rope that I know *has* to be there. It's about pulling myself up, inch by inch, second by second, until a sliver of light that I know *has* to be there, flickers above me.

That's my optimism. I wish I could go back and tell that reporter that m*y* optimism is an *action* word. Something I work at, not something I *have*. And it's tied up in one big, hot mess with persistence and faith. It's not always pretty, and it's not always perfect.

Mom is scurrying around my room, packing my bag. I hear a familiar voice down the hall.

"Lexi, I'm gonna find you!"

I squeal like I'm five again. My door flings open.

"You were always terrible at hide-and-seek," Tucker says.

After hugs and kisses, Tucker picks up my juice box from my tray and drains it. I arch in protest, and we both laugh.

"Why don't you show Tucker around the floor while I finish up?" suggests Mom.

He rolls me *responsibly* to the door. When we cross the threshold, he pops a wheelie and races me down the hall.

After three laps, we roll back in the room, both of us breathless. Mom is gone but my packed bag is on the bed. My garland is neatly folded and resting on an oversized envelope.

I point to my cookie sheet.

Tucker picks it up. "This old thing?"

"Yeah," I say.

Tucker shakes his head. "It's Hannah who's good at this. Not me."

I point again and say, "Eees!"

He sighs. "I'll try. But only because you asked nicely."

He puts the board in my lap and hunches over me, holding my wrist.

I spell, **What if this doesn't work?**

I've thought it a zillion times, but I haven't had the courage to say it until now. To get through the last few weeks, I've made myself focus on potential, but now that we're starting act three of my play, the question has become more persistent.

I think back to that Aha! moment I had while clinging to Hannah's back at Monkey Joe's all those years ago: *All this time I've been looking for more, but what if . . . what if this is all?*

It'll be months, maybe years, before we know for sure. I think I have to consider both possibilities.

Tucker shrugs. "What if? It's not like it's the end of the road. It's not over until you say it's over. You're in charge, re-member?"

I laugh. I know how many times in the last few months I have insisted—demanded—that I am in charge. But the funny thing is, the more control I've been given, the more I think I don't actually have it. Maybe it isn't anyone's to give away.

Tucker looks at me with his head tilted, like he's thinking he might ask me what's so funny, but instead he stretches out on my bed and scrolls through his phone.

Mom comes back with the nurse. "We were going over the discharge form, and I thought you would want to sign it yourself."

"Yeah!"

My arm flies out and pumps until Mom wrangles it in. She holds the pen in my hand. I sign my name. It's official. Tucker throws my bag over his shoulder. He spins me into the hall and pops a wheelie. I laugh so hard I can barely breath. The nurse clears her throat.

Before she can say anything, the elevator door opens, and Tucker wheels me inside. I fling out an arm and press 1.

Downstairs, we pass the chapel, the cafeteria, the lab. We roll outside to bright Kansas City sunshine.

And on to the rest of my life. My voice. My story.

EPILOGUE
Age 15

It's been two years since surgery, and although I am still in Act Three, a lot has changed. For one thing, my body is starting to listen to my brain more. A lot of the time, I can keep my head upright, and sometimes I can even sit in my wheelchair without a vest strapping me in. I have more reliable control of my eyes too.

My voice—my actual speaking voice—is a little stronger and still improving. Don't get me wrong, it's still hard to understand me, and I'm *beat* after a few words, but I think with more time and practice it will get even better.

I've also come a long way on Haha. My eyes still aren't fast enough to use her in regular conversations, but I have written some of my school papers on her. I'm using her more and more for writing. It's hard work, but I'm ninety-nine percent sure that someday I will be Lexi Haas, published author. Scratch that. If you're reading this, I'm one-hundred percent sure.

I've also figured out how to email, watch YouTube videos, and play Candy Crush on Haha (yeah, that last one is a rabbit hole and gets me in trouble with Mom on a daily basis). Oh, and I can web surf! Check this out: wookietranslator.com. It's exactly what you think. You type in a phrase in English, and it spits it out like a Wookiee would say it. Tucker is trying to figure out how to connect it to Haha so I can really talk like Chewbacca.

I'm still struggling with ways to make my computer voice sound like *me*. Mom and Celeste are working on it. They've found an organization that uses donated voices to make computerized speech sound more like a human and less like a machine. They're trying to find out how I can get one. I want mine to have a British accent, but Dad says that people will think I'm adopted. Can you see me rolling my eyes right now?

The really cool and exciting thing is the new technology that's coming. Right now, there are companies perfecting interfaces that will allow me to send my *thoughts* to a computer, and the computer will speak them for me. Do you know what this means? All my mental telepathy practice might *actually* come in handy. Someday, I'll be able to just think, *Go ahead. Scratch. Your. Butt.* and my computer will say it. Crazy, right?!

But let's talk about *friends*. Anna and Elle have both started regular school, so I don't see them as often these days. Even with our different schedules, we still get together to do movies and hang out. In the last couple of years, I've had the chance to share my story at conferences and meetings with doctors, lawmakers, and families. In the process, I've made loads of new friends—people who can understand better than anyone because they live with kernicterus too. But Anna and Elle will always be the first. Any time I need to remember that, I squeeze my imaginary rock. *Obviously.*

So that pretty much brings us to *today*. Right now, we're at the beach! Nearly my whole family is here. Kali couldn't come because of her grad school schedule, and yeah, The Cat stayed home, but everyone else made it. Can you believe my parents actually sprang for an entire weekend this time? We didn't even bring coolers.

Yesterday, I splashed in the waves in my new beach wheelchair. In this chair, I can roll right out into the water. We also rolled down the sand and collected shells.

Gus loves to jump in and out of the waves, but I think he's ready to get back home to his cat. Lucky for him, because today we have to head back to Charlotte.

Before we go, there's one more thing I want to do. One promise I need to keep.

"Are you ready?" Dad asks.

"Yeah!" My voice is loud and steady.

"Everybody knows their part, right?"

We all groan because we've been over this like fifty times.

"Okay, then. One. Two. Three."

Mom lifts me up to stand in the sand, and everyone else grabs an arm or leg.

"Now, you have to lean forward and push off your hand," Dad instructs.

But I know how to do it. I have done this literally a thousand times—in my head.

I lean forward. Dad guides one hand onto the sand. Kasey puts my other hand beside it. Tucker and Hannah lift my legs up and over my head. Finally, Mom pulls me up by the waist, and before I know it I'm upright again. The head rush afterwards is, I admit, unexpected.

But I did it. My perfectly imperfect, family-assisted cartwheel.

Everyone cheers—me, my family, even random people walking down the beach all stop and clap. I whoop and laugh and wobble a little. Or maybe a lot. Then I point to the sand. I'd like to do another one. *Obviously.*

To Our Readers

A letter from Susan

The Year of the Buttered Cat is based on the true story of Lexi and our family. Lexi and I began working on this years ago as a homeschool writing project. Lexi has always loved reading, so I wanted to give her the experience of putting her thoughts on paper to share her unique perspective. Our first stories were retellings of real things that happened in Lexi's life that were funny, or incredible, or touching.

When we decided to put all the stories into one book, many scenes were compressed and timelines altered. Some scenes have combined events from various times in her life. In other cases, we have added or changed details to make a connected story. A few scenes, like the epic Nerf blaster battle, were completely made-up. However, the story of how Lexi's voice was stolen when a doctor failed to monitor her newborn jaundice and the two pioneering surgeries she underwent to try and get it back is entirely true.

Lexi really does have a Facebook page with thousands of devoted and caring fans. And yes, much to my family's horror, I really did butter The Cat.

Our process of working together to create stories has not changed over the years. Lexi gets her main points across with a combination of spelling and talking, and once I understand her idea, I ask her yes/no questions to narrow down and further define the scene. The task of putting all this information together onto a page—including word choices, sentence construction, imagery, and other writing considerations—is mine. As you might guess, it's a painstaking process to make sure every page reflects Lexi's true thoughts and opinions.

Lexi is getting better at using Haha, and we're excited about new advances that can help give her, and others like her, a stronger voice. There is even a way you can help. We recently learned about the Human Voicebank Project, a service that matches donor voices with people who use augmentative communication devices. By donating a sample of your voice, you can help give an actual voice to someone who can't speak. To see how you can become a donor, please visit www.vocalid. co/voicebank.

I asked Lexi to tell me about her hopes for this story. Her answer is below. As for me, I hope her story will help spread the word about the importance of monitoring newborn jaundice.

Most children won't have the devastating problem Lexi experienced, but all new babies with jaundice need to have their bilirubin levels tested and plotted on the Bhutani nomogram (http://lexihaas.org/bhutani/) to see if they are at risk for developing kernicterus.

I also need to acknowledge the founding families of Parents of Infants and Children with Kernicterus (PICK), who first sounded the alarm to the medical world about the dangers of newborn jaundice two decades ago. I also want to thank Dr. Steven Shapiro, Dr. Vinny Bhutani, and the late Dr. Lois Johnson for their tireless work in preventing and treating kernicterus. You can learn more, or even donate to Dr. Shapiro's research, at kernicterus.org. A portion of the proceeds of the sale of this book will be donated to the Kernicterus Research Center.

From Lexi:

My entire life, I have loved books. They help me jump realities in a way nothing else can. There is nothing more amazing than climbing into someone else's skin and experiencing a completely different life for an afternoon.

I hope that by sharing my story, you can begin to understand what it's like to live in a body like mine. My life may be very different from yours, but do you remember the part where I said I don't want to be you? *True*. I *like* who I am, and many of my friends with physical challenges and other disabilities feel the same way.

In so many ways, I am incredibly lucky. First, I have always been surrounded by people who believe in me. Family, friends, therapists, and thousands of Facebook fans I have never even met have encouraged and cheered me on. Also, I have already had many opportunities to "be the evidence." I have been invited to spread that message to doctors, parents, and policymakers, educating them about kernicterus and newborn jaundice.

If there's one thing I hope you will take from this book, it is that people with disabilities—even severe ones—have interesting internal lives and a lot to offer as friends. We probably even have a lot in common with you. My hobbies are YouTube bingeing, listening to books, and then watching the movie adaptations (I almost always like the books better), crafts (when I can help and not just watch someone else do them), swimming, horseback riding, and hanging out with friends. I also love UNC basketball—Go Heels! And of course, I still love all things superhero and high action! In school, my favorites are literature, mythology, and history. How about you? Do you think you could be friends with someone like me?

Letter from Dr. Steven M. Shapiro:

I hope you have enjoyed reading this book and getting to know Lexi. I have known Lexi for most of her life—ever since her mother brought her to see me when she was a baby. Like many of the children I see in my clinic, Lexi has kernicterus.

You read in the *The Year of the Buttered Cat* that bilirubin inside a newborn's body makes skin and eyes yellow, or jaundiced. Most babies have some jaundice from slightly elevated levels of bilirubin. This mild jaundice in newborn babies is normal and not dangerous. But sometimes the level of bilirubin in the blood gets too high and gets into the brain. This can be dangerous. It can damage parts of the baby's brain and cause what Lexi has, kernicterus.

Most of the time when bilirubin gets too high, babies act sick. They get very sleepy and do not nurse well. They may arch their heads and spine backwards and have muscle tone that goes from very stiff to very floppy. Often these babies have an unusual high-pitched cry and are unable to move their eyes upward. It can look very scary! Their parents bring them to the emergency room, not because they are jaundiced, but because they are sick.

When bilirubin starts to get too high, the hospital can put these sick babies under special lights, bili lights, to help their body get rid of bilirubin. When bilirubin gets extremely high, a special type of blood transfusion can quickly lower their bilirubin. But sometimes these treatments are not done or are not done soon enough. Those babies—like Lexi—may then suffer with the lifelong condition of kernicterus.

Lexi's case was a little unusual because she did not seem sick enough to need treatment at the hospital, but her bilirubin was still high enough to cause kernicterus. If her doctor and medical team had done a simple blood test to check her bilirubin level, they would have known it was too high. She could have been treated before it became dangerously high and caused brain damage. There are good guidelines for when to treat with the special bili lights and when to treat with the special blood transfusion. There are even guidelines to predict which jaundiced babies need close monitoring so their bilirubin levels don't get too high. Lexi's bilirubin was too high and went untreated for three weeks because her doctor didn't think it was a problem.

High bilirubin damages parts of the brain that control hearing and movement. Some kids with kernicterus have a type of deafness called auditory neuropathy that causes distortion of sounds. Some kids, like Lexi, have movement disorders. Some kids have both. But in all of these kids, the thinking part of their brain works fine. Many of these kids are very smart, just like Lexi. They often have a great sense of humor and are very observant. They are regular kids in bodies that don't work well for them.

It is important to know that not all babies who have jaundice will get kernicterus. Only a very few have so much jaundice and bilirubin that it is dangerous. By testing early and often with a blood test or a special skin sensor these babies can be treated to prevent permanent lifelong damage. Newborn jaundice needs to be *managed* to make certain that all babies have the same chance for a normal life. Doctors and nurses, medical providers, and parents need to be educated about jaundice and bilirubin and know how to follow simple guidelines to test for and prevent kernicterus. Everyone should know about it and help spread the word about testing newborns to prevent kernicterus from happening.

As a pediatric neurologist, I am glad I can help families and their children manage their kernicterus. I do research to learn better ways to detect and prevent it. But, in the future, I hope you and others in the public will be informed, ask questions, and also help prevent this preventable form of brain damage. If you would like to read more, please visit my website at www.kernicterus.org.

About the Authors

Susan Haas is a Charlotte, NC-based medical writer, dog lover, and painfully slow runner. She's the number-one fan of her five adult kids and husband, Ken. Most days she would gladly trade the family cat for a Starbucks latte.

Lexi Haas is very much the spunky, sassy, superhero-obsessed teen in *The Year of the Buttered Cat*. She embraces her inner nerd, her love of a good romance story and her disability but if you stand too close to her wheelchair, she will pinch you.